Dear Reader:

The book you are about to read is the latest bestseller from St. Martin's True Crime Library, the imprint *The New York Times* calls "the leader in true crime!" Each month, we offer you a fascinating account of the latest, most sensational crime that has captured the national attention. *The Milwaukee Murders* delves into the twisted world of Jeffrey Dahmer, one of the most savage serial killers of our time; *Lethal Lolita* gives you the *real* scoop on the deadly love affair between Amy Fisher and Joey Buttafuoco; *Whoever Fights Monsters* takes you inside the special FBI team that tracks serial killers; *Garden of Graves* reveals how police uncovered the bloody human harvest of mass murderer Joel Rifkin; *Unanswered Cries* is the story of a detective who tracked a killer for a year, only to discover it was someone he knew and trusted; *Bad Blood* is the story of the notorious Menendez brothers and their sensational trials; *Sins of the Mother* details the sad account of Susan Smith and her two drowned children; *Fallen Hero* details the riveting tragedy of O. J. Simpson and the case that stunned a nation.

St. Martin's True Crime Library gives you the stories *behind* the headlines. Our authors take you right to the scene of the crime and into the minds of the most notorious murderers to show you what really makes them tick. St. Martin's True Crime Library paperbacks are better than the most terrifying thriller, because it's all true! The next time you want a crackling good read, make sure it's got the St. Martin's True Crime Library logo on the spine—

Charles E. Spicer, Jr.
Senior Editor, St. Martin's True Crime Library

Patricia Ramsey rose early the next morning, the day after Christmas. There was, she knew, much to do before her family would be ready to leave. It would only be a short trip to the vacation home near the shores of Lake Michigan. After that it would be back to Colorado, where her daughter JonBenét would compete once again, this time, of all things, in a Little Miss Hawaii pageant.

Patsy wrapped herself in her robe as she descended the circular staircase from the third floor, where she and her husband, John Bennett Ramsey, had their gigantic bedroom. She would make the coffee, as she did most mornings. It wasn't that the Ramseys could not afford to have a cook, or even live-in servants; the fifteen-room brick Tudor often seemed more house than was necessary. But Patsy believed very deeply, even religiously, in things like family values, and one of her beliefs was that a family that did things together, even mundane things like making coffee, was a stronger family.

Near the bottom of the staircase, approaching the first floor, Patsy saw three pieces of yellow paper lying on one of the steps. She bent down to pick the pages up.

"*Mr. Ramsey,*" the first page began. "*We have your daughter.*"

Death of a Little Princess

The Tragic Story of the Murder of JonBenét Ramsey

CARLTON SMITH

St. Martin's Paperbacks

DEATH OF A LITTLE PRINCESS: THE TRAGIC STORY OF THE MURDER OF JONBENÉT RAMSEY

ISBN: 0-312-96433-1

Printed in the United States of America

St. Martin's Paperbacks edition/September 1997

10 9 8 7 6 5 4 3 2 1

ACKNOWLEDGMENTS

The killing of a small child is always a traumatic event, an event that resonates with everyone. We see in our children that unique combination of hope and innocence that promises the world of the future will be better than that of the past; when that promise is betrayed, we all feel as if we have lost something that can never be replaced.

That was how it was with JonBenét Ramsey. She came into our lives smiling, dancing, singing, posing with just the slightest suggestion of coquettish innocence that made us smile as well. Surely, we thought, no one could be so base as to rob such a delightful child of her very life.

But someone did, and we wanted to know who it was, if for no other reason than to feel that such horrors should never go unresolved. What follows here is a description of the events surrounding JonBenét Ramsey's death, and how it became, for both good and ill, a national obsession.

Special thanks are necessary in accounting for the preparation of this book under very tight time constraints. Charles Spicer and the staff of St. Martin's Press were marvelous in pulling this project together under difficult circumstances. Former FBI agent Robert Ressler's counsel was invaluable. Finally, a number of friends in Boulder—you know who you are—will always be remembered for their advice and friendship. Thanks to all.

Carlton Smith
February 1997

Death of a
Little Princess

CHRISTMAS, 1996

The icy wind lanced down from the high Canadian plains, curling down along the eastern front of the Rockies. By late afternoon the cold air rolled up to the jagged gray, brown, and green shards called the Flatirons, just south and west of Boulder, Colorado, and then ran into a warm front still lingering there after a sunny Christmas Day. The cold air rose, the warm air followed it, and just before five P.M. snow began to drop softly, silently from the darkened skies.

By six P.M. the city of Boulder was being dusted by a fine white coating—a trace, as the weatherpeople called it, of a white Christmas. By eight that night, the snow was deep enough to register footprints. And then it stopped. The cold wind slackened, and the people of Boulder turned up their furnaces to settle in for the night. Or most of them, anyway.

*   *   *

Patricia Ramsey rose early the next morning, the day after Christmas. There was, she knew, much to do before her family would be ready to leave. It would only be a short trip to the vacation home near the shores of Lake Michigan, but in three days it would be Patsy's fortieth birthday—the big Four-Oh, everyone called it— and she was looking forward to spending the New Year's holiday with her summer friends along the snowy shore of Lake Michigan. After that it would be back to Colorado, where her daughter JonBenét would compete once again, this time, of all things, in a Little Miss Hawaii pageant.

Patsy wrapped herself in her robe as she descended the circular staircase from the third floor, where she and her husband, John Bennett Ramsey, had their gigantic bedroom. She would make the coffee, as she did most mornings. It wasn't that the Ramseys could not afford to have a cook, or even live-in servants; the fifteen-room brick Tudor often seemed more house than was necessary. But Patsy believed very deeply, even religiously, in things like family values, and one of her beliefs was that a family that did things together, even mundane things like making coffee, was a stronger family.

Near the bottom of the staircase, approaching the first floor, Patsy saw three pieces of yellow paper lying on one of the steps. She bent down to pick the pages up.

"*Mr. Ramsey*," the first page began. "*We have your daughter.*"

And then, in one of those moments when time seems to stop, the heart of Patsy Paugh Ramsey, former Miss West Virginia, about to be forty, the happy wife of a successful businessman, was shattered by a bolt of terrifying, unthinkable fear, the first step down the road that would alter her life forever.

Quickly Patsy raced back up the staircase to the second floor, then down the hallway to JonBenét's room. Her daughter wasn't in her bed.

"John! John!" Patsy called out, as she pumped furiously back up the staircase once more, this time to get her husband, who was just getting out of the shower. Quickly Patsy showed him the three yellow pages. John glanced at the words, then ran down the stairs to the second floor to see for himself. It was true. JonBenét wasn't in her room. John and Patsy went to Burke's room. Nine-year-old Burke was safely asleep in his bed, but JonBenét wasn't in that room either. John and Patsy now made a frantic search of the whole second floor, then the first. JonBenét was nowhere to be found.

Now John Ramsey looked closer at the yellow sheets. The words were cryptic, yet very threatening. The handwriting was in block letters made by a black felt-tip pen. There were references to John's business and a recent bonus his company had given him. There were words about foreign interests and terrorists. There was a reference to John's own career in the Navy, a year he'd spent at Subic Bay in the Philippines. John, the words said, would have to pay $118,000 to get JonBenét back—the exact amount of his recent bonus. There was something about an attaché case for the money. And, the words went on, John should prepare himself for a very strenuous ordeal. Most chilling, there was a frightening threat: unless the demands were met, JonBenét would be . . . beheaded. Under no circumstances, John was advised, should he call the police.

That was exactly what he was not going to do. In fact, Patsy was already making the emergency call. At 5:52 A.M. the 911 dispatcher for the Boulder Police Department picked up the telephone, and the world at large for the first time heard about the kidnapping of a six-year-old beauty queen named JonBenét Ramsey.

"Send help," Patsy pleaded. "Send help."

Kidnapping remains the rarest of American crimes, far less frequent than murder or even kidnapping's first cousin, extortion. In 1995, the last year national statistics were compiled, the Federal Bureau of Investigation recorded only a small handful of kidnapping for ransom cases, as opposed to nearly 22,000 homicides.

The reason for the disparity between murder

and kidnapping is simple: kidnapping is an extraordinarily difficult crime to successfully commit, if the measure of success is the actual collection of a ransom demand.

The primary reason for this is the efficiency of the police in the United States. The point of contact between the ransomer and the person demanding the payoff is critical; in effect, it provides the authorities with the opportunity to follow the kidnapper or his accomplice and thus identify them; from that point, it is a relatively simple procedure to recover the victim and effect the arrest.

The Boulder Police Department, while hardly used to kidnapping as a routine, nevertheless knew what to do. Within a few minutes a patrol car was on the way to the Ramsey house, in the fashionable Chautauqua Park neighborhood of Boulder. A call was placed to the local FBI agent, since the FBI would have jurisdiction in any kidnapping case, and especially if the kidnapper had taken JonBenét across a state line. Arrangements were made to assemble telephone taping and tracing equipment for the call the kidnapper had promised to make.

As the Boulder police were organizing, the Ramsey family was making more telephone calls, this time to friends in Boulder. A minister was called, along with a friend who was a lawyer and the family doctor. Thus, by the time Boulder police detectives arrived in force at the scene of the Ramsey house, the dwelling was already crowded with a number of extraneous people.

There are two primary objectives for a police agency faced with a kidnapping. One is, obviously, to recover the kidnap victim unharmed. The other is to apprehend the perpetrator. And in a case where the perpetrator has promised to contact the source of the expected payoff—in this case, John Bennett Ramsey—the opportunity arises to play with the mind of the perpetrator: to feed information, to recover some, to sense the perpetrator's psychology and background. It's a bit like playing a fish on the line; strike too soon and the fish is gone forever, the lure discounted. But lay enough line, reel in artistically, and the fish will come into the creel. This would be the task of John Bennett Ramsey; it would be up to him, coached by the authorities, to discern the essential difference between being a victim, as the kidnapper had perceived him, and being a hunter—someone capable of using the contact with the kidnapper the way a fisherman might land a trout.

While the equipment was being set up, the police took a cursory tour of the house, paying particular attention to the exterior doors. Already, someone had noticed footprints in the snow outside. Yet there were no signs of breaking and entering—no broken doorjambs, splintered by pry-bars, no broken glass. There was no forced entry, which seemed to suggest that from the beginning the kidnapper had good connections, possibly someone inside who had let him or her in. Or perhaps: was the kidnapper a dweller of the domicile, someone who knew the layout of the fifteen rooms, who knew where JonBenét's bedroom was, who knew Patsy's routine, and the custom of the early morning coffee-making?

And the house's security system had given no warning of any intruder, which was another piece of evidence. The conclusion was obvious: no break-in, no intruder. This was no Lindbergh case, not with the evidence as it was being discovered, with no ladder leaning against the exterior wall, no clear sign that malefactors had forced their way into the Ramsey house.

Indeed, the house alarm was not turned on, even as the police inspected it.

What did that mean, if anything? Had the kidnapper somehow defeated the alarm system? Had the Ramseys even turned it on?

Arrangements were made to assemble the $118,000 ransom demanded by the kidnapper. The ransom was to be in $100 bills, as specified. Now there was nothing to do but wait for the kidnapper to make contact. But that was when things began to go haywire.

In the midmorning, several new FBI agents arrived from Denver. The fact that the ransom note made references to foreign interests raised the possibility that terrorists might be responsible for the kidnapping, an added reason for the FBI's involvement in the case.

Also arriving at the house were several members of the Boulder County district attorney's office, and it was at that point that trouble began. Later, the sequence of events would prove controversial. Some said that the police asked John Ramsey for permission to search the house thoroughly, but that John refused to give this permission. It may have been, however, that John was taking advice from his lawyer friend, Fleet White, and that White might have suggested that police observe all the legal fundamentals by formally requesting a search warrant.

Accordingly, the representatives of the district attorney's office sought and obtained a search warrant for the house. The warrant was delivered in the early afternoon. But before the warrant was executed—that is, before the police began their officially sanctioned search—it was suggested by the detectives that John Ramsey make his own thorough search first. Accompanied by Fleet White, John Ramsey descended to the basement of the house, which had been partitioned into several rooms.

Pushing open a door into an unfinished wine cellar that had previously been used to store the family Christmas presents and Christmas decorations, Ramsey and White encountered the huddled form of little JonBenét, covered with a blanket. Her mouth and neck were covered with gray duct tape. A nylon cord was wrapped around her neck, and twisted tight by a wooden stick used for leverage. A second cord was tied to her wrist.

"Oh, God, no, no!" John Ramsey moaned. He quickly bent down and removed the blanket, then pulled off the duct tape around JonBenét's mouth. He prayed that JonBenét was somehow still alive. Swiftly he scooped his daughter into his arms and raced back up the stairs to the living room. JonBenét was put on the floor near the Christmas tree, where the doctor immediately determined that JonBenét was dead, and had been for some time. Besides being strangled by the nylon cord, the left side of her skull had been crushed by some heavy object. It was likewise clear that she had been sexually assaulted, because traces of blood and signs of bruising were clearly apparent.

It was too much for Patsy to think about. Only the night before she'd put little JonBenét in bed, after one of the happiest Christmases of her too-short life. Now she was gone, suddenly and ferociously ripped out of the world by some unfathomable evil, someone or something that had crept into the heart of the family in the dead of night. The thought of JonBenét's terror during her last minutes alive was more than anyone could think about, least of all her mother. Patsy was given drugs to calm her down and hopefully to help her sleep. The Ramseys' friends made arrangements for the family to leave the house immediately while the police, perhaps belatedly, executed their search warrant. It would be the last time Patsy would ever be inside that house, the scene of a horror that would forever, to her, make the dwelling itself seem like an artifact of living evil.

THE GOOD SHIP
LOLLIPOP

———

The pictures were haunting, as well as disturbing, at least to some.

Here was a little girl, elaborately costumed, posing provocatively, dancing somewhat suggestively, singing a song, "I Wanna Be a Cowboy's Sweetheart." Here were closeup shots of a little girl's face, lips painted ruby red, eyes exquisitely made up, gazing into the camera with alluring promise. Here was another shot, of a tiny seductress, dressed in white feathers, in a gold-starred bodysuit with just the suggestion of padding around the chest area, moving bare arms and legs in practiced motion, evocative of a Las Vegas showgirl in full cavort.

In the days following the discovery of JonBenét's battered body, these were among the images of her that flooded the nation and the world, along with a listing of JonBenét's titles: 1996 Little Miss Colorado, Colorado State All-

Star Kids Cover Girl, America's Royale Little Miss, Little Miss Charlevoix, National Tiny Miss Beauty. And almost as quickly as the images swirled into public consciousness, the inevitable leap of logic was made: that these activities were somehow connected to JonBenét's murder.

In what was to be a foreshadowing of the events of the entire murder case, it was almost as if there were two JonBenét Ramseys: the one seen so frequently in the plethora of professional still photos and amateur videotapes, the professionally amateur beauty queen who would go on singing and dancing, frozen forever in eternity as a six-year-old prodigy; and the other, real JonBenét, the flesh-and-blood little girl so wantonly abused by something or someone from the lower depths of depravity. In the fine line between fame and notoriety, it was the Little Miss who would go on living, however unfairly or inappropriately.

Under the circumstances—as people grappled with the notion of just what had happened—it was inevitable that the entire idea of child beauty pageants would come under scrutiny and debate in the media-made town square of Village America, where, thanks to the marvels of electronic communication, the events in a small Colorado town can be made to seem as if they are happening right next door.

There were, on one side, those who deplored

the contests that had made JonBénét so famous as clear exploitation of children.

"It's impossible to look at these photos and not see a terribly exploited little girl," Denver Chief Deputy District Attorney Karen Steinhauser observed, in a lavishly illustrated (exploitative?) spread on the murder case published by *People* magazine. "You get this uncomfortable, sad feeling that she didn't get the chance to be a normal, six-year-old kid."

But Steinhauser's observation included the key, operative phrase: "You get this . . . feeling." In truth, it was actually impossible not to look at the images and not project one's own feelings onto the pictures.

Because, on the other side of the question, was the assertion by child beauty pageant defenders: that the contests, far from exploiting children, taught them such valuable intangibles as poise, self-confidence, charm, and style, thereby equipping them for a world that prizes such qualities, particularly in women, more than almost any others.

And there was the *New York Times* columnist Frank Rich, who came down squarely on the anti-pageant side of the furious national debate when he observed, in a column titled "Let Me Entertain You," that the media's very fascination with JonBénét's life and death was itself a piggy-backing onto the pageants' "pre-pubescent prurience" that had hithertofore "provoked no outrage from the moral guardians who hold press conferences every time there's a new Calvin Klein ad campaign . . ."

Rich's point was telling: that many of the same people who clamor for family values were those who defended the beauty pageants as a wholesome experience for children. Rich went on to estimate that the child beauty pageant business—which is exactly what it is, with the ever-hopeful parents paying the tab—is today a $1 billion-a-year industry. There are more than 3,000 pageants and up to 100,000 contestants each year. And it is fair to note, this industry is mined industriously by costume designers, photographers, media consultants, dancing and singing coaches, and the pageant operators themselves, some of whom clear $100,000 on the fees and licensing associated with their productions.

Rich touched on one of the most striking aspects of the beauty pageant business—the fact that most of the contests are held in the South, the clear bastion of the family values movement. To Rich, this smacked of the worst form of hypocrisy; but in fact, it might be argued that what this really illustrates is a far more profound, even historic, clash between the cultures of the North and South.

Why are beauty pageants so much more prevalent in the South than the North? One answer might be discerned in Colonial America. Where the original colonists in the northeast came largely from Puritan stock, followers of Oliver Cromwell and the anti-Catholic Roundheads, those in the tidelands of the south came in the main from English landed aristocracy, and were backers of the Restoration of Charles II. Where the Puritans of the Massachusetts Bay Colony eschewed colorful clothing and piously constricted their manners to be humble in the sight of God, the planters of the South valued chivalry and style that tended to place womanhood on a pedestal. Class was everything in the South, whereas in the North, all classes were to be equally humble before God.

For a woman born in the South, dressing well, developing the subtle manners of charm and beauty, of using those talents as the means to succeed, was natural. But it was the very reliance on those skills, being so assiduously inculcated in Little JonBenét, that troubled so many feminists from the North. It was the very values themselves that so troubled the feminists: be sexy, be provocative, sing a little song, do a little dance, and you too can be somebody.

"If a girl is put into the position where she is told that her worth is measured by her looks and her ability to entertain, the message comes across very strongly that that's all she's worth," Regina Cowles, the Boulder coordinator for the National Organization of Women, told the *Daily Camera.*

Perhaps more insidious is the reality that such pageants produce winners—and losers. The message, claimed critics, was that girls could be ranked, in effect, sorted out, by surface characteristics such as beauty or talent, thereby focusing a child's pattern of growth and development toward the superficial image. And beyond that was an even more disturbing notion: that success for women in modern America lay primarily in the idea that the projection of an image allowing someone to appear desirable was the ticket to fame and fortune, an implicit recognition that manipulation of male desires was the sure pathway to success. It was, in effect, the same as telling a black child that the surest pathway to success was to be an athlete or an entertainer, and just as ghettoizing.

And there were real questions of the lasting damage such assumptions could create. To be told that one doesn't measure up to the arbitrary standards of beauty and talent can, for some children, be devastating. If you're an also-ran in something evidently so highly prized by society at large, it can be depressing and lead to a loss of motivation for other pursuits, and indeed, even a loss of self-confidence or self-worth.

Even the winners can experience problems.

"From a mental health standpoint," Colorado psychiatric social worker Libby Bortz told the Denver *Post*, "it's not conducive to developing inner and outer [strength] when you're simply rewarded for one part of your being. It can lead to a loss of humanity in people who are very narcissistic."

In extreme cases, this narcissism can lead in

later years to drug addiction, eating disorders, and even suicide.

Beyond the effects on a child are questions about the effects on adults. There are some, for example, who believe that the dressing of small children in adult costumes, with adult make-up and dance routines, only feeds an underlying current of pedophilia. In addition to purposefully stoking such notions in the minds of normal adults, there is the prospect that such pre-pubescent packaging could prove highly attractive to practicing pedophiles.

"They're an attractive package for somebody to violate a young person," Ted Cohen, president of a Miami-based directory of pageants, told the Denver *Post*. "The girls are certainly in a situation where they're in the limelight for [someone] looking for that type of person to abuse. It's a great temptation for people who are beyond control of themselves."

And there are the effects on the parents. The prospect of pageant success can lead to visions of a fantastic future filled with huge sums of money from commercials, movies, fashion modeling, and other forms of entertainment. One only has to look at the television for a few hours to see how prevalently the images of young children are used to both sell and entertain. It would be unreasonable for the parent of a successful pageant child not to contemplate such possible rewards as they simultaneously if unconsciously begin to view their child as a marketable commodity rather than a child. Such expectations can have a deleterious effect on the parent-child relationship. "If the child loses," Cohen told *Time* magazine, "they feel like they let the parent down."

And there is yet another aspect of the pageant business. For some parents, getting involved in the beauty competition can be like playing with living dolls—literally. The child can become an expression of the adult's own need for glory and approbation. The child can become a prop for the parent.

"The question is, at what age can a child decide for herself?" Boulder's Cowles told the *Daily Camera*. Cowles thought she knew the answer to that question, at least as regarded JonBenét. "This girl—six years old—can barely cross the street by herself."

But again, there seem to be two JonBenét Ramseys, each of which emerged into the glare of personal projection. For every critic who called the image of JonBenét in red lipstick and high heels disgusting or "salacious," as some did, there were just as many who saw nothing wrong with JonBenét making such rapid progress toward a career as an entertainer—no different than a Tiger Woods learning how to play golf at the age of four or Mickey Mantle lying in his crib with a baseball.

It does seem clear that Patsy's involvement in JonBenét's budding career was reflective or her own success in the same arena. Whether

JonBenét would have chosen this path if left to her own devices is unclear. What is clear is that Patsy had been down the path herself, and it had been very good to her. In some respects, to say that Patsy wanted JonBenét's success more for herself than for her daughter is to be cruelly unfair; it was, in the deepest sense, a mother's love for her daughter, and wishes for her future happiness, that led to the limelight that was to tragically become so lurid.

PATSY

Patricia Ann Paugh was born December 29, 1956, in Parkersburg, West Virginia, the older daughter of Nedra and Don Paugh, an engineer for Union Carbide. Parkersburg was a small town of 34,000, located on a broad southeastern turn of the Ohio River, just over the river from the state of Ohio. One of the city's claims to fame is the Federal Bureau of Public Debt Building, a legacy of the federal budget legerdemain of West Virginia Senator Robert Byrd.

By all accounts, the Paugh family seems to have been typical of their time and place. Don Paugh was a capable engineer, and the family seems to have been grounded in middle-class values of work, discipline, and success. For Patsy and her younger sister, Pam, success meant being socially adept and, some thought, making oneself attractive for the right man. Good works in the community were valued, along with special talents. The family was fundamentally religious and prized the values of family life.

Even so, those who knew Nedra recalled later that Nedra was very involved in first Patsy, then Pam, going into the beauty pageant circuit. Patsy was a slender, green-eyed brunette, capable of bringing herself off with style and grace. While still a sophomore at Parkersburg High School, she became the first runner-up in the Miss Teen-Age West Virginia contest.

Patsy's success in the pageant competition appears to have encouraged her to continue. As a sophomore at West Virginia University in Morgantown, Patsy was a contestant in the Miss West Virginia contest. Finishing as a runner-up in two contests, in 1977 Patsy finally won as a contestant-at-large. That gave her a shot at the big one: the Miss America contest.

The potential career benefits of winning the Miss America contest in a culture as steeped in the virtues of sex appeal as America can hardly be overstated. Winners are almost immediately afforded the opportunity for lucrative modeling and acting careers, which if nothing else lead to plentiful opportunities to come into contact with successful men. Patsy's career as a Miss America contestant was dominated by her discipline and determination. There was, some recalled later, plenty of practice, practice, practice—in walking, declaiming, learning how to smile and wave. At the same time, Patsy learned how to see herself as she wanted others to see her—the mark of a skilled performer.

"From the minute you arrive in Atlantic City," Patsy was later to recall, "you're exposed to a barrage of reporters and photographers watching your every move and every word."

At the 1977 Miss America pageant, Patsy won one of the non-finalist talent awards for a dramatic reading.

Still, the discipline and practice may in fact have handicapped Patsy in that it made her seem, to some at least, *too* practiced. The writer Frank Deford, a judge of the 1977 Miss America contest in which Patsy participated, was to recall that while Patsy was a good speaker, she seemed a bit too programmed for his taste. He noted at the time, perhaps a bit too cruelly, that she seemed "a little automaton," Deford told *Newsweek* several weeks after JonBenét's murder. This seems to be an echo of later characterizations of JonBenét's own presence on the stage, which seemed over-controlled to some pageant observers. Photographers praised JonBenét's ability to hold a pose, certainly an unusual talent for a six-year-old, and it's likely that this was a skill JonBenét learned from her mother at an early age.

At West Virginia University, Patsy chaired the Student Services Committee, and served as the membership chairperson for her sorority, Alpha Xi Delta. She earned a degree in journalism with an emphasis on advertising, and she made the dean's list. What many people remembered about Patsy, apart from her charm and good humor, was her deep religious convictions. She was, some recalled later, very devout in her Christianity.

Two years after Patsy was a Miss America contestant, so was her younger sister, Pam. It was the first time in the history of the pageant that two sisters had competed.

After graduating from West Virginia in 1978, Patsy took an advertising job in Atlanta. It was there, the following year, that John Bennett Ramsey observed her going into an apartment building and was smitten. Ramsey resolved to track the unknown woman down, and did so. Within a year, they were married. He was thirty-seven, she was twenty-three.

JOHN

By the time he saw the then twenty-two-year-old Patsy going into that apartment building in Atlanta, John Bennett Ramsey had already lived another lifetime.

Born in 1943 in Nebraska, one of two sons of a decorated U.S. Army Air Corps transport pilot, John Ramsey grew into adulthood in Michigan, where his father, James "Jay" Ramsey, served as director of the Michigan Aeronautics Commission. Jay Ramsey ran Michigan's airports with such an iron hand that he soon earned the nickname "Czar" Ramsey.

The elder Ramsey's passion for order, method, and discipline appears to have been passed on to John.

In high school in Okemos, Michigan, a small town not far from Lansing, John Ramsey was seen by others as quiet, determined, and extremely well organized. John played in the school band, ran cross country, and was the chairman of the school's Christmas dance in his senior year.

"Everything he did demonstrated character," John's former classmate, Nancy Turner Lawson, told the *Rocky Mountain News*. "He was just an upright person who had a desire to do things right. He had a savings account. He had a plan for his life. I can't tell you how responsible he was at eighteen."

After leaving high school, John enrolled at Michigan State University in Lansing. There he became president of his fraternity, Theta Chi, joined the Reserve Officers' Training Corps, and earned a degree in electrical engineering. It was at Michigan State that John met his first wife, Lucinda, who was majoring in elementary education. A month after both graduated in June of 1966, John and Cindy were married in Cindy's hometown of Kalamazoo.

Shortly after the marriage, John entered the Navy to fulfill his ROTC commitment. Following the path of his father, John became a naval aviator. During his tour of duty, from March of 1968 to November of 1969, John was stationed at the Navy's Public Works Center, part of the Subic Bay Training Command at the sprawling Navy base in the Philippines.

After leaving the Navy, John and Cindy returned to Lansing, where John obtained a master's degree in marketing. By this time, John and Cindy were the parents of their first child, Elizabeth.

After earning the master's degree, John accepted a job with an electronic engineering company, and he, Cindy, and Beth, as the baby was called, moved to Atlanta, Georgia. Another daughter, Melinda, was born in 1973, and then a son, John Andrew Ramsey, in 1976.

It was shortly after John Andrew's birth that things began to change for John and Cindy. First, the electronic engineering firm wanted John to move to California. But John refused to go.

"That was the turning point for me," John later told a trade publication, *Computer Reseller News*.

It was a turning point for all the Ramseys, as it turned out. In 1977, John and Cindy separated. They were divorced the following year. In the settlement, Cindy received the Ramsey house, a nearly new Oldsmobile stationwagon, and custody of the three children: Beth, then eight; Melinda, six; and John Andrew, a little over a year old.

It was a little over a year after the divorce—the same year that Patsy graduated from West Virginia University—that John first saw Patsy and decided to find out who she was.

John married Patsy on November 15, 1980 at the Peachtree Presbyterian Church in Atlanta. By the time of the wedding, John had formed his own company, Advanced Products Group, to sell computer terminals, printers, and similar equipment from an office in the basement of his house.

Now, seventeen years later, it's difficult to recall a time when computers were considered mere novelties, certainly not the backbone of office productivity or home entertainment that they have since become. No one at the time except for a few visionaries ever foresaw the day when a substantial portion of American homes would have desktop computers linked to something called the Internet or that computers would be reduced so far in price and size as to be most business travelers' frequent companion.

But John Ramsey, merging his electronics engineering background with his degree in marketing, was at the right place at the right time: the world of computer hardware and software sales was about to explode.

John didn't manufacture the computers; instead, he specialized in selling and setting up the equipment for businesses. In effect, John became a sort of middleman between the computer manufacturer, like International Business Machines, and the end user, such as a car dealership wanting an accurate record-keeping system for sales, commissions, inventory, maintenance, taxes, and the like. John's company specialized in fitting the machine and the software to the customer, taking a commission from the latter and getting a volume discount from the former.

As computer systems rapidly became more sophisticated, demand for higher-end systems— computers capable of processing vast amounts of information quickly—began to expand as well. The faster a computer could calculate, the more information it could process; this in turn led to the design of systems capable of such complex tasks as industrial designing, aerodynamic modeling, sophisticated mapping, and intricate engineering. All of these tasks required a display system capable of graphically illustrating what was being designed, mapped, or engineered. What was more, as changes were entered into the computer, the changes would immediately be reflected in the graphic image of the design displayed on the computer screen.

This was called computer-assisted design, or CAD in the acronyms so beloved of computer designers. By the middle 1980s, such high-end CAD computers were being marketed as "workstations," and were often used by engineering companies, architectural firms, graphic designers, and eventually, by animators and movie special-effects experts. These machines might cost anywhere from $10,000 to $50,000. Many were made by Sun Microsystems, a Mountain View, California, computer manufacturer that used sophisticated software based on UNIX, a powerful programming computer language. Among companies providing the design software was another California company called Silicon Graphics.

About the same time as demand was beginning to grow for these sophisticated systems, the hardware and software manufacturers began to find themselves overburdened by maintaining a separate sales force. Decisions were made to contract the sales and distribution ends of the computer businesses to firms specializing in that sort of thing. Advanced Products became what would soon be termed a value-added reseller, or VAR, in that John's company would handle sales, distribution, and service of the sophisticated CAD systems to the end customer, the computer user.

But by the end of the 1980s, the number of such value-added resellers was too large for efficiency, and economic pressures began to force consolidations. In late 1988, John merged Advanced Products Group with two other companies, CAD Distributors of Boulder, Colorado, and CADSources Inc. of Piscataway, New Jersey. The new company would be called Access Graphics Technology, Inc., and would be based in Boulder.

For the first two years, things did not go smoothly.

"We managed to turn three profitable companies into one large unprofitable one," John told the *Daily Camera* in 1993. But after reorganizing, the enlarged company began to steady down, and in the fall of 1990, the company scored a masterstroke when Sun Microsystems, the big workstation manufacturer, designated Access Graphics as its principal sales and distribution outlet for nearly two hundred value-added resellers; in effect, that made Access Graphics sort of a super reseller—called a "master reseller." From then on, a little less than two-thirds of the Sun systems resellers would have to go to Access Graphics to get the product and the servicing. Under the agreement, Access was to buy computers ahead of demand and build up an inventory, which would permit far faster supply for many of the resellers. It also netted Sun a nice chunk of immediate cash, relieved the manufacturer of some of its more burdensome costs, and gave Access Graphics a dominant position in terms of naming prices for the Sun systems, since it controlled much of the supply.

This was a major step forward, and Access's sales figures began to shoot upward. The company had sales of around $50 million a year when it began; by 1993, the sales figure had reached $400 million.

John was the vice president of sales and spent much of the first two years of the company's existence in the air, in his own airplane commuting between Atlanta and Boulder. By this time, Patsy had given birth to Burke. Three years later, just before Sun made its momentous decision to make Access the master reseller, JonBenét was born, as well.

The difficulties of managing sales in the newly merged company created conflict; and in the end, it was John who prevailed. Named the company's president in 1991, John decided to give up the frequent flying and move his new family to Boulder.

BOULDER

The spectacular, sharply tilted shards of gray and brown rock festooned with patches of green fir called the Flatirons—for their resemblance to the same when placed on end—are called foothills in Boulder, although they look like mountains to most people from the far flatter South, like Atlanta.

The place that the Ramseys would now call home was a sharp cultural break from the slower, warmer rhythms Patsy and John had known for so long. For one thing, Boulder was nearly all white. It was also affluent—very affluent, as well as very liberal.

The town itself has developed a reputation for insularity. There was, for example, a bumper sticker that read, "BOULDER: SEVEN SQUARE MILES OF VIRTUAL UNREALITY." Indeed, the city's officials and its guiding lights appear eager to eschew any vulgarities associated with such sordid activities as murder. In the aftermath of Jon-Benét's killing, the mayor and chief of police hastened to point out that "the incident"—as they referred to it—had been Boulder's only murder of the year.

The modern Boulder is amply provided with bicycle paths, including special underpasses to permit riders to cross the town's few expressways. Open space, particularly along Boulder Creek, which bisects the town, is common. Cultural amenities abound, as do restaurants; in fact, Boulder has many more restaurants than churches. Smoking is considered gauche, and can't be committed anywhere in public in the town, except outside, and even then is greeted by nasty frowns. Conservatives in Boulder are moderates everywhere else; the town voted 87 percent for Bill Clinton in the 1996 election. Many of the residents are caught up in various progressive causes, such as saving the rain forests and combating world hunger, and meetings and petitions are the order of the day.

Long a bucolic university town, Boulder has also been for some time a major gateway to recreational areas in the Rockies. Mountain recreation—skiing, snowshoeing, rock climbing, hunting, and fishing—can be found in abundance within a relatively short distance from town. All of these sports require money—for skis, for snowmobiles, for climbing equipment, for four-wheel-drive vehicles, if one is so inclined. As a result, Boulder has become a sort of jumping-off spot for the affluent on their way to the woods.

With these characteristics, and blessed with clean air, year-round sunshine, good schools, and very little crime, Boulder became a natural mecca for low-polluting, high-tech companies like as Access Graphics. Such Information Age companies employ bright, well-educated people and pay them well. Not needing a railroad line or wharf to market their products, or much in the way of raw materials, the Information Age company can pick its location based almost entirely on where it believes its employees will be most comfortable. Thus, companies like Access Graphics end up in places like Redmond, Washington, or Scott's Valley, California, or Hillboro, Oregon—places generally out of the big city, surrounded by a clean, natural environment, and handy to outdoor recreational pursuits so frequently favored by their young, upscale employees.

At its inception, Boulder began in the shadow of the Flatirons, the spectacular outcroppings that front two larger mountains behind them, Bear Mountain and Green Mountain. There were, in the beginning, two main streets: Broadway paralleled the southeastern curve of the mountains before heading due north, and Pearl Street, the main commercial thoroughfare, which crossed Broadway while it was still on its curve, heading slightly west-southwest by east-northeast. In the southeastern quadrant formed

by the two crossing streets the state of Colorado
had erected the University of Colorado, home of
the Buffaloes. The university's 20,000 students
today add a colorful mixture to the town's population, and cause seasonal fluctuations in traffic jams and various disruptions, very few of
them incidents.

Across Broadway to the southwest, in gridlike
patterns heading up the gentle rise toward the
Flatirons were some of the older and more substantial homes in the town, among them a
house purchased in 1991 by John and Patsy
Ramsey.

Many of these houses were made of red brick.
Surrounded by pines and patches of lawn, the
houses gave the very picture of a quiet, peaceful,
slightly quaint old-time family neighborhood—
the sort of place where one knows the mailman
by name, where kids might toss a ball in the
street without getting run over, and where everyone knew everyone else.

Despite this, Patsy wasn't entirely comfortable in the new town, at least initially. She missed
Atlanta, her house, and her activities and family
there. If people in Boulder were friendly, they
were in a way that seemed different than the
people in Atlanta. Many of the people in Boulder
were, like the Ramseys, comparatively new ar-
rivals. Some of them, in fact, seemed a little
snooty. There was less of the openness that was
prevalent in the South, and one always had the

sense that people were holding something back in Boulder.

But Patsy had not been a Miss America contestant for nothing, and she threw herself into socializing in Boulder with determination. She volunteered to assist at Burke's new elementary school, and she and John both supported Boulder civic activities. As JonBenét grew, Patsy began spending more and more time with her daughter—dressing her up, taking her to pageants, enrolling her in classes—and in the process, meeting more and more people. Bit by bit, the ice began to melt.

John, meanwhile, was quite busy with Access Graphics. The firm had opened a headquarters in downtown Boulder on the Pearl Street Mall. Thanks to the deal with Sun, business was booming. About the time John became president of Access, Lockheed Martin, the giant aerospace company, bought the remaining seventy-five percent of the Access stock. Lockheed's purchase of twenty-five percent of the company in 1989 had given Access the necessary cash to make the deal with Sun; now Lockheed would own the whole thing. John became a director of Lockheed Martin.

The success of the business enabled John to achieve many of his fondest dreams. In 1992, the Ramseys bought a $300,000 vacation home in Charlevoix, an affluent resort town on upper Lake Michigan. John kept a sailboat, *Miss America*, and a powerboat, at nearby Lake

Charlevoix. In Boulder, John became an investor in a popular restaurant, Pasta Jay's.

By 1993, Access Graphics was by far the fastest growing business in Boulder. Sales were leaping upward at an astonishing rate. The company bought a four-story building on the mall, a former rock-and-roll dance hall, and converted it to office space. Employees at the headquarters had mushroomed from fifty to 170 in three years.

By 1996, the company had blasted off. John had been named Boulder's "Entrepreneur of the Year" by the city's Chamber of Commerce in 1995. Laurie Wagner, the company's spokesperson, estimated in October of 1996 that Access would have sales of nearly $1.2 billion—twenty-four times larger than the 1988 sales. The company now had 380 employees in Boulder, and expected to have 470 by the end of 1997. The company worked out plans for a ten-year expansion program to occupy still more buildings on the Pearl Street Mall. The company had established operations in Europe, Canada, and Mexico City.

Meanwhile, Don Paugh, Patsy's father, had retired from Union Carbide and joined Access as vice president in charge of operations. Access might be owned by Lockheed, but running it was becoming a Ramsey-Paugh family affair.

Not long after their arrival in Boulder, the Ramseys set about remodeling the two-story brick Tudor they acquired for around $500,000 in 1991. Extensive renovations were made, including the addition of a third floor where John and Patsy had a bedroom later said to be 1,500 square feet in size. The circular staircase was added, as well as a separate catering kitchen for parties. Patsy loved parties. All in all, the house was 6,866 square feet in size when the renovations were done. There were fifteen rooms. The renovations and additions had made the floor plan somewhat convoluted. There were corridors that seemed to dead-end and corners where they wouldn't ordinarily be expected. The renovation bill alone, newspapers in Colorado reported, was around $700,000. One of the renovated new rooms was in the basement: a wine cellar used as storage, with a single naked light bulb hanging from the ceiling and windowless walls. The door usually stuck, and there was no wine.

PROBLEMS AND QUESTIONS

The loss of any child is painful for any parent, but the loss by murder is worse by far. That the child should be murdered in one's own house, on such a traditionally happy family day as Christmas, is almost too emotionally laden to contemplate.

And yet, there in the early afternoon of December 26, lay the little body of JonBenét Ramsey—beside the Christmas tree, no less. An ugly, terribly evil Christmas present. Someone found a blanket or sheet to cover the little form.

Under the circumstances, it hardly seemed the right time to interrogate John and Patsy. What time did you last see your daughter? Did you hear any screams in the night? Those weren't the sort of questions the Ramseys were in any condition to answer, and reasonably enough, the Boulder detectives and FBI agents agreed with the Ramseys' friends that the Ramseys should be taken out of the house as soon as possible.

Once that was accomplished, the detectives could begin to work.

The most important task facing them was the need for a thorough search of the house. It seemed clear that the murder had to have occurred someplace in the house, but where? Had it taken place in the empty wine cellar? Or somewhere else? What evidence could be found to show where the murder occurred?

Another problem was likewise immediately apparent. John Ramsey's removal of the body of his daughter from the wine cellar had disrupted the evidence. His action was completely understandable under the circumstances. What was puzzling, to outsiders at least, was why police had allowed him to search the residence unaccompanied by a police officer. Had a detective been present when John made the grisly discovery, the detective might have prevented John from disrupting the scene.

Every murder has its own telltale clues, often microscopic in nature. Moving the body can disrupt or dislodge those microscopic pieces of evidence, such as fibers, drops of fluid, hairs, dirt, or paint flakes. Additionally, each time a surface comes into contact with another surface, there is often a transfer of particles between surfaces. Thus, it now seemed quite likely that fibers or other microscopic bits from John Ramsey had been transferred to the body of JonBenét. The problem the detectives would have to face was determining whether any such transfer occurred *before or during* the murder, rather than when John discovered the body.

Equally serious, John's action in removing the body before it could be viewed and photographed as the killer left it prevented the detectives from reconstructing just how the killer had behaved when the killer had placed the body in the room. Quite frequently the position of the victim when left by the murderer is an indication of the killer's mental state at the time of the crime. Now they would only be able to rely on the descriptions given to them by John and Fleet White.

These were investigative problems faced by Sergeant Larry Mason, Boulder's lead detective, placed in charge of the case by John Eller, commander of the city's detective division. But if there were investigative problems, there were also numerous questions about the crime.

Who, for example, would have known to put the ransom note on the staircase routinely used by Patsy? Who could have gotten into the house without the Ramseys' knowledge? Who knew where JonBenét's bedroom was? How had the writer of the ransom note known about John Ramsey's $118,000 bonus? And why that amount? Ramsey was capable of raising a far larger ransom. Why only $118,000?

These and other similar questions arose quickly in the minds of the investigators. Indeed, the peculiarities of the ransom note only begged the question: had there really been a kidnapping attempt at all?

There were really only two basic possibilities: that a kidnapping attempt had somehow gone wrong and ended in murder, or that the ransom note was simply a blind, an attempt at misdirection, to prevent anyone from immediately searching for and finding the body—that the murder had come first, followed by a bogus ransom note, authored in an attempt to cover up the crime.

Or there was another thought: was it possible that someone outside the house had committed the murder and authored the ransom note in some sort of attempt to implicate John Ramsey as the murderer, by referencing things particular to John Ramsey's background, like his $118,000 bonus or the reference to Subic Bay? Even that seemed to indicate intimate knowledge; in the note the reference was to "SBTC," the initials, not the complete name. Was this all some form of bizarre and extreme revenge on John Ramsey, payback for some real or imagined injury or slight?

The questions were growing larger by the minute, and until the search was completed, there could be no answers, only speculation.

But as the afternoon wore into the evening, the case began to assume very strange proportions.

"It's not adding up," Boulder County Assistant District Attorney Bill Wise told the *Rocky Mountain News*.

The news of JonBenét's horrible death broke across Boulder and most of Colorado the following day. It all seemed, at first, very tragic. It wasn't until later, when all the photographs and videotapes of the dancing and singing JonBenét hit the airwaves that it was to become a national obsession. By that time, even stranger things had happened, however.

The Boulder officials tried to get ahead of the media curve. In the beginning it was easy. A press conference was called for Friday, December 27, at the city's modern Public Safety Building, just as the Boulder County coroner John Meyer released preliminary results from an autopsy of JonBenét. Death, Meyer said, was due to asphyxiation. JonBenét had been strangled.

Boulder detective commander John Eller conducted the news conference. A large color portrait of JonBenét, smiling and with blond hair in ponytails, was pinned to the wall behind him.

Eller was long on promises but kept the details short.

"It's still very delicate and sensitive," Eller said.

"The family," Eller said, "has been cooperative and our investigation is continuing."

Now the questions came pouring in.

Why didn't the police search the house immediately?

"We had no reason to believe the child would be in the house at that time," Eller said.

What was in the ransom note?

"The ransom note was a typical—if there is such a thing—a typical kidnapping ransom note, the kind you'd find in any movie."

How much was demanded in ransom?

Eller wouldn't say.

What was JonBenét wearing? Had the body been hidden or left in the open? Who found her?

Eller refused to answer those questions too.

Had kidnapping been ruled out, then?

No, said Eller, and then displayed a remarkable talent for mixing double-negatives. "We have no reason not to believe that it was, or not, at this time," he said. To clarify he added, "It's too early an investigation to start ruling things out."

Had John and Patsy been interviewed?

Not exactly, said Eller.

"The parents are going through a tremendous grieving process," Eller said. He said detectives wanted to let that go forward, and that they intended to "work our interviews" around the Ramseys' grief.

"It is truly a tragedy," Eller said. "This is a beautiful young girl, as you can see. Very vibrant, and from all reports that we have at this time, very precocious, a wonderful child."

After the news conference, the media fanned out through the Ramseys' neighborhood. This first time, neighbors were eager to talk. It wouldn't last very long.

A number of reporters encountered Joe and Betty Barnhill, who lived across the street from the Ramsey house, and helped take care of JonBenét's little dog, Jacques. The Barnhills had attended a party at the Ramsey house on the Monday before Christmas. Betty Barnhill characterized Patsy as generous and very friendly.

A reporter for the *Daily Camera* asked Joe Barnhill if he'd seen anyone over at the Ramsey house on Christmas Day.

"I didn't see a lot of people over there Christmas Day," Barnhill told *Camera* reporter Elliot Zaret. He'd seen Burke ride a bicycle on the lawn. And, he said, he'd seen John Andrew Ramsey, John's son from his first marriage and a student at the University of Colorado, come to the house.

"As far as I know," Barnhill told the *Rocky Mountain News*, "John wouldn't have any enemies who would do a thing like this to him."

As Barnhill talked with reporters, police were still busy at the Ramsey house. By that afternoon they were photographing and taking measurements of the footprints in the snow—the footprints that had to have been left after eight p.m. on the night of the murder.

By Sunday, December 29, police had run out of information they were willing to impart about the murder. As a result, the news media, anxious to have something new for their Sunday editions and programs, turned to the usual reliable sources: official leakers, unidentified family friends, and the neighbors.

Those same neighbors would soon grow heartily sick of the reporters, especially the television people, with their trucks, their intrusive camera tripods, and their blow-dried reporters asking questions designed less to obtain facts than to elicit emotional reactions. But this was still the beginning, before the media blizzard, as *Los Angeles Times* television critic Howard Rosenberg was later to describe the invasion.

"Mystery shrouds murder," the Denver *Post* headlined. "Details still elusive in slaying", said the *Daily Camera*. There was really nothing new to say, but because people—readers, viewers, *customers*—demanded more information, the story was rehashed.

Joe Barnhill was trotted out once more. He talked of having kept JonBenét's Christmas bicycle at his house until 9 P.M. Christmas Eve, when John had claimed it to put under the tree. Some of the reporters took a turn at playing detective. Barnhill and others were asked who besides the Ramseys had access to the house.

Oh, there were plenty, the reporters were told. There was a housekeeper who came in three times a week, sometimes with her husband. There were cooks and caterers and handymen and remodelers, a whole string of people coming and going much of the time. Some thought as many as ten or fifteen people might actually even have keys to the house.

Barnhill was now invited to be the detective and guess what might have happened. He didn't know, Barnhill said, but maybe, just maybe, John Ramsey's business success, or maybe JonBenét's shortlived beauty pageant career, had brought a criminal's unwanted attention.

"Who knows what that psychotic person is going to do next?" Barnhill told the *Post*. "Sometimes it does not pay to be in the limelight."

A KILLER ON THE LOOSE?

JonBenét's body was released by the coroner on Sunday, December 30, and a two-hour memorial service was held at St. John's Episcopal Church in Boulder. Afterward, the Ramseys took JonBenét's casket and boarded a corporate jet that flew them to Atlanta.

Joe Barnhill continued to brief reporters.

"The person had to be acquainted with the interior of the house, because they knew where to hide the body," he told the *Post*.

That seemed fairly clear, especially when the police announced that they were still searching the residence. The many rooms and corridors, police said, were making a thorough search a complex task. The subtext was that maneuvering around inside the darkened house in the middle of the night would be difficult for a stranger.

"It's still wide open," said Sergeant Mason, the

lead investigator. "We've got theories and ideas, but we don't have a suspect. It's been really difficult. This one is damn tough."

One fact was reported: the investigators had obtained hair, blood, and handwriting samples from John, John Andrew, Melinda, and Burke, as well as several friends of the family. But a formal interview of John and Patsy had not yet taken place, and no samples were taken from Patsy, City of Boulder Director of Communications Leslie Aaholm said.

"They've been grief-stricken and not in any condition to be interviewed," Aaholm told reporters. She said no one had been ruled in or out as a suspect.

The following day, an emotional funeral service for JonBenét was held at Atlanta's Peachtree Presbyterian Church, the same place where John and Patsy had been married sixteen years before, and where JonBenét had been baptized in 1990.

It wasn't the first time John had attended a funeral in the church for one of his children. More than four years before, his firstborn daughter, Beth, had been killed with her fiancé, Matthew Dellington, in a snowy traffic accident in Chicago while both were on their way to meet Matthew's family. It would have been Beth's first encounter with the family she would never get a chance to marry into.

JonBenét's small casket was covered with pink flowers, and a small white teddy bear sat next to it, bearing silent witness to the fact that JonBenét wasn't coming home again. The Reverend Frank Harrington, who had baptized JonBenét, spoke.

"When a child is lost," said Reverend Harrington, "one feels that a part of a future promise is gone." JonBenét had been taken by "cruelty and malice, by some unworthy person or persons. I can tell you that the heart of God is broken by the tragic death of JonBenét Ramsey.

"JonBenét's life has ended, but as long as we live, she will be alive in our memories."

A soloist sang the Lord's Prayer, and as the verses rose, so did Patsy, raising her black-gloved hands to the heavens in a charismatic beseechment for God's grace.

"We're going to sing now, and we can cry as we sing," Reverend Harrington said, leading the congregation into the simple Christian children's hymn of "Jesus Loves Me." At the end of the hymn most of the congregation was in tears.

Afterward, Patsy, John, Burke, and the rest of the family placed long-stemmed, yellow roses on JonBenét's casket. Four pallbearers carried the casket out of the church to a waiting hearse, and the long ride was made to the St. James Episcopal Cemetery in Marietta, where Jon-Benét was buried next to the older half-sister she barely knew, Elizabeth. Patsy lingered at the grave, touching the flowers left behind on her daughter's casket, and then she and her family drove away.

But on the same day that JonBenét was being buried, a bombshell of sorts was dropped.

John and Patsy had hired criminal lawyers.

Bryan Morgan, a well-known Denver criminal defense attorney, confirmed that he'd been retained by John Ramsey.

"The district attorney," Morgan told the *Post*, "has said no one is ruled out."

Had Morgan advised John not to talk to the detectives?

"I have zero to say about what I have told or not told my client," Morgan told the paper.

Why was John hiring a criminal lawyer? In a culture so steeped in police mythology, from reality television shows to the mystery movie of the week, claiming the right to talk to an attorney seems, to the unsophisticated, tantamount to an admission of guilt. "What do you need a lawyer for if you've got nothing to hide?" comes the query.

When a police agency is attempting to find evidence leading to the conviction of a murder suspect, and the murder victim is a close relative, found in your house, under circumstances that strongly suggest that the murderer had to be familiar with both the victim and the layout of the dwelling, one doesn't take any chances that the police may make a serious error. That's simply good legal advice: rights must be protected, for the innocent as well as the guilty.

In ensuing days, a great many comparisons of

the JonBenét Ramsey case would be made to
two other high-profile crimes that transfixed
America: the O. J. Simpson murder prosecution
and the Olympic Park bombing.

The O. J. Simpson case would be invoked
when news media and other critics soon began
to fault the slow pace of the Boulder police investigation into JonBenét's death. The police,
stung by the criticism, responded that they
wanted to take all the time necessary to make
sure of their evidence before making any move
to arrest anyone. They did not want to "O.J. the
case," as the Boulder *Daily Camera* was to report. They did not want to act precipitously and
make errors, either charging the wrong person,
or worse, letting the right person get away because of sloppy police work.

The Olympic Park bombing case was likewise
instructive, at least as far as John's decision to
hire a criminal lawyer. When the Olympic Park
bomb went off, it was only a few days before security guard Richard Jewell was viewed as a
suspect by the Federal Bureau of Investigation.
It later turned out that Jewell's rights were vio-
lated by the Bureau. Had Jewell not had a lawyer almost from the beginning, the possibility
existed that Jewell might have been wrongfully
convicted. The FBI and the Department of Justice later cleared Jewell of any complicity in the
crime.

For John, having a lawyer to make certain
that the police cut no corners, jumped to no

conclusions, rushed to no judgments, was simply good sense. And for the police, waiting on every last bit of possible evidence—and a substantial amount was being collected from the house—was likewise good sense.

Beneath the surprise of John and Patsy's decision to retain counsel, however, another fact dribbled out: John Andrew had been in Atlanta on the night of the murder, as had his sister Melinda. Both had been visiting Cindy and her husband.

Apparently Joe Barnhill had been wrong about seeing John Andrew at the Ramsey house on Christmas Day. Unnamed "authorities" said that both of John's children by his first marriage were out of the city of Boulder at the time of the crime. But Boulder communications director Leslie Aaholm continued to insist that no one had been ruled in or out as a suspect so far. Contacted by the Denver *Post*, Joe Barnhill declined to speak, saying he'd been asked by police to stop giving interviews. Barnhill added that the request had come through the police from the Ramseys.

By this time, some of the neighbors were beginning to show the first signs of impatience with the media onslaught.

"We, as neighbors, really prefer to respect the dignity and privacy," one told the *Post*. "This is a horrible situation. There's not a thing we could say that we know that would help."

But if the neighbors were buttoning their lips,

the following day brought another surprise: John and Patsy went live on CNN.

Some thought Patsy might still have been under medication. The exhaustion of grief was obvious. Sometimes she appeared to slur her words. She and John held hands as they responded to forty minutes of questions from CNN reporter Brian Cabell, reporting from Atlanta. During the course of the interview, John and Patsy provided details about the crime that had not yet been published or officially confirmed: that duct tape had been placed over JonBenét's mouth, and that she had been strangled with a cord.

Cabell set the interview up by observing that in cases of child homicide, "it is very normal police procedure to look at the family, first of all, as possible suspects in this case." Cabell told the audience that John and Patsy understood this, and accepted it.

Early in the interview, the Ramseys contradicted Boulder communications director Leslie Aaholm, who had said that police had obtained no blood, hair, or handwriting sample from Patsy. John said that wasn't true, that every member of the family, including Patsy, had provided the samples. Cabell asked Patsy if she had given the samples, and Patsy nodded.

Then occurred one of the quirks of journalism, the sort of nonsequitur, intentional or inadvertent, that has the effect of sending public perceptions in an entirely different direction, thus influencing the news coverage and requiring the police to respond in what perhaps was an unplanned fashion.

Although Boulder police and city spokeswoman Aaholm had insisted from the beginning, as had Boulder County District Attorney Alex Hunter, that no one had been "ruled in or out" as a suspect, Cabell now used a question to report something that no one had yet said, at least officially:

"The police said a couple of days ago," Cabell began, "to assure the other residents of Boulder, 'There is no killer on the loose here, you can be assured everything is under control.' Do you believe that someone outside your home . . . ?"

"There is a killer on the loose," Patsy responded. "I don't know who it is, I don't know if it's a he or a she, but if I were a resident of Boulder, I would tell my friends to keep—" and at this point Patsy's voice broke.

"It's okay," John said, trying to comfort her.

"—to keep your babies close to you," she finished. "There's someone out there."

The sequence of this exchange may in fact have been crucial, at least as far as the relationship between the Boulder police and the Ramseys in subsequent weeks.

Where did Cabell come up with the notion that there was "no killer on the loose?" In retrospect, it appears that it may have sprung out of the sound-bite reporting that so characterizes journalism in the Electronic Age. Looking back, it appears that the phrase "killer on the loose" was first uttered by an unidentified Ramsey neighbor several days earlier, who said she feared that a "killer was on the loose" and was quoted in a newspaper article.

Just how the phrase moved from an expression of fear to a denial by the police was unclear. Perhaps Cabell had asked police for a response to the neighbor's concern and had received assurances that there was "no killer on the loose."

But if Cabell had reported this, he was the only one. None of the three Colorado newspapers covering the case had carried such denials; they kept reporting police were saying "no one had been ruled in or out," which presumably included a "killer on the loose."

The import of Cabell's question was clear: if police believed there was "no killer on the loose," that had to mean the police had an idea of who committed the murder. That in turn focused scrutiny on the people who had been in the house at the time of the murder—John, Patsy, and Burke. Thus did the Ramseys become public suspects in the death of their own daughter, a development which was to have significant consequences later.

Cabell pressed on, saying that the FBI did not "necessarily" regard the case as a kidnapping attempt. The Ramseys responded that the note, the ransom demand, the promise to safely return JonBenét if the money was paid sounded like a kidnapping attempt to them. And John added that if authorities didn't believe a kidnapping had been attempted, it would concern him.

"Because," he said, "if we don't have the full resources of all the law enforcement community on this case, I'm going to be very upset." John then said he intended to hire his own investigators and experts to find out who committed the crime, and that he would put up a $50,000 reward for information leading to the arrest and conviction of the killer.

Cabell tried again to turn the focus back on the Ramseys.

"Inevitably," he said, "speculation on talk shows will focus on you." Then came the softball setup, giving the Ramseys their cue: "It's got to be sickening."

"Oh," John said, "it's nauseating beyond belief."

And it was, in more ways than one.

The Ramseys' CNN interview had an immediate impact back in Boulder. Colorado newspapers reported that the Boulder police were "surprised" by the Ramseys' interview. Boulder police chief Tom Koby refused to comment on Patsy's remark about a "killer on the loose."

"I'm not going to respond to the comments of a grieving mother," Koby told the *Daily Camera*. All he knew, Koby said, was that someone who killed a little girl had not yet been apprehended.

The idea of a serial murderer, some stranger capable of breaking into residents' houses in the dead of night to spirit their children away to basement rooms to be sexually assaulted and murdered, did not sit well with Boulder officialdom.

"City officials denied that there is any immediate threat to residents," the Denver *Post* reported. "'I think we need to be careful, but I don't think there is a crazed murderer looking for the next victim,'" said Mayor Leslie Durgin. "'Obviously somebody killed the girl, so there is obviously a killer on the loose. The police have assured me they have met with neighbors. They are advising caution for parents of young children, but they always do.'"

Leslie Aaholm made it even more clear: "Police don't feel there's some strange person in Boulder they need to be worried about," she told the *Rocky Mountain News*. And in her own remarks to the *News*, Mayor Durgin drove the point home ever further.

"There is a killer," she said, "but I think the implication, which is completely erroneous, is that there is a murderer walking up and down the street looking for young children." That was wrong, Durgin said, pointing out that there was no forced entry, and that the killer appeared to know the layout of the house. To her, Mayor Durgin said, that did not imply a random act.

There it was: the Ramseys believed their family had been attacked by an outsider, while the authorities kept insisting that there was no cause for the general public to be alarmed, tantamount to saying there was no outsider.

Thus did the compass of public opinion waver from east to west, before finally settling back on the magnetic north of the Ramsey family. If there was no outsider, it had to be an insider. And who was inside? The Ramseys.

In the aftermath of the interview and response by city officials, reporters began digging deeper into the Ramsey family. Soon reporters began tracking down old neighbors, housekeepers, business associates, a former nanny, college fraternity brothers of John Andrew, and inevitably, the Paughs back in Atlanta, where John and Patsy had returned to seclusion.

TO THE PRESS: NO COMMENT

The day after city officials' response to John and Patsy's interview, Boulder and Atlanta had both become scenes of frenetic news media activity, a situation worsened when it leaked that a team of Boulder detectives had flown to Atlanta on New Year's night to inquire about the Ramsey family's background, thus establishing two separate locales to whipsaw the story.

Nearly two dozen out-of-town reporters flew into Boulder, including representatives of *Good Morning America,* the British Broadcasting Corporation, and the shock troops of American journalism, the checkbook-bearing supermarket tabloids. Boulder residents soon began to complain of media overkill.

The *Daily Camera* sought out a talking head to explain just why all these reporters had come to Boulder.

"Children die all the time," Jan Whitt, a journalism professor at the University of Colorado, told the paper. What made the story different, she said, was a national fascination with the troubles of the wealthy. It was that, she said, along with a normal dearth of news that usually accompanied the Christmas and New Year holidays.

Soon the word "elements" was in the air. "Elements" is a word journalists like to use when they try to explain why they're doing what they're doing, as in, "The story has all the elements."

In the case of the Ramseys, the "elements" were a precocious and beautiful young beauty queen, a mysterious murder in a lavish family home on the night of the biggest holiday of the year, a wealthy family, and most of all, the flood of photographs and amateur videotapes of JonBenét posing and performing, which soon flooded the visual media and the magazines as those with the images rushed forward to cash in. With such a mixture of elements, the story of JonBenét's life and death was seen as irresistible to the information-consuming public.

Meanwhile, some Boulder residents continued to express fear that a killer was "on the loose" and questioned the efforts of the Boulder police, which added yet two other "elements"— the possibility of a serial killer preying upon the talented children of the rich and the concurrent possibility that the Boulder police were too incompetent to do anything about it. Some residents wanted to know what was taking so long and why the police were being so tight-lipped, if indeed there was "no killer on the loose."

Mayor Durgin weighed in again: "The police," she said, "have the responsibility to not only solve a murder but to get a conviction. It is not to feed the media news, it is not to satisfy entertainment of the talk radio."

The mayor said the Boulder police didn't want a reprise of the "O.J. Simpson trial, and I support them in that."

Spokeswoman Leslie Aaholm released a statement the day after the Boulder officers arrived in Atlanta, saying that the city's detectives "were completely taken by surprise by the Ramseys' interview [on CNN], but have no comment . . ." The detectives, Aaholm said, would interview members of the Ramsey and Paugh families, friends, and gather background information.

"The officers have been authorized to approach the family to schedule an interview with them in Boulder at a later time."

Aaholm added that police "concur with Mrs. Ramsey's statement [on CNN] that she has provided police with hair, blood, and handwriting samples." This seemed to hint at one reason why the Ramseys had hired lawyers: if the city had disseminated erroneous information that Patsy had not submitted to the tests when she had, perhaps it was better that counsel be available to keep the city on the straight and narrow.

Beyond Boulder, activities by press and police alike soon centered in Roswell, Georgia, a small town about fifteen miles north of Atlanta. The Paughs lived in Roswell, and the Ramseys were staying with them. While the Boulder detectives set up shop at the Roswell Police Department, the news media rushed to the Paugh house in mobile units and set up camp, which in the news business is referred to a "stakeout," but which is actually closer to stalking. The street in front of the Paugh home was soon clogged with media vehicles, including television satellite trucks. If the Boulder police suddenly swooped down on the Ramseys to make an arrest, no one wanted to miss it. The Paughs put a handwritten sign on the front door: "To THE PRESS: NO COMMENT."

Virtually all of the national news media, including CNN, the Associated Press, *Newsweek*, *People*, the *New York Times*, the national broadcasting networks, and the supermarket tabloid forces were on the Paughs' street. As usual, they tended to clump together in a herd for safety: if one outlet got a break, everyone wanted to know about it, so everyone watched everyone else, and, also as usual, traded rumors and gossip.

The Paugh neighbors were disgusted with the behavior of the media in the stakeout. "Vultures!" one hissed. "Haven't you learned anything from Richard Jewell?"

"You're sick!" said another. "Why don't you get a life?"

As the afternoon wore on, some clumps of the media blob detached themselves to shadow the Boulder detectives around town, following the officers in their own vehicles to see who they talked to, the better to set up their own later interviews to find out what the cops had asked about. Nothing much came of any of this, although several former acquaintances said the police had asked whether any of the Ramsey children had ever been abused, a possibility that was roundly hooted as ridiculous by those interviewed. The Ramseys' former nanny in Roswell, Shirley Brady, told the *Post* that the idea that John and Patsy were suspects in Jon-Benét's murder was "about as useful as a screen door on a submarine." The detached clumps of the media gravitated back to the Paughs, where later on Thursday evening, January 2, the Ramseys made a break for it, jumping into a van with tinted windows to race to the airport and a private flight back to Boulder.

Meanwhile, new details about the murder had begun to leak out in Boulder, probably from police sources in response to the Ramsey CNN interview. The *Post* on Friday, January 3, reported that the cord around JonBenét's neck—"Like a parachute cord," the paper said—was tied with a slip knot around her neck, and that the cord had a piece of wood at the end which could be used as a handle to tighten the noose. The paper also had discovered that both JonBenét's neck and mouth had been covered with duct tape, with the cord tightened around the neck on top of the duct tape.

More significantly, it was reported that the Boulder County Sheriff's Department, assisting the Boulder city police, had borrowed a sophisticated machine called an Omniprint from the Arvada, Colorado, police department. The Omniprint used a laser light source to pinpoint difficult to see substances on other surfaces—such as small semen stains, saliva, blood drops, and sometimes even fingerprints that ordinarily were not apparent to the naked eye. The laser and its mirror measured distances between surfaces so precisely that it was possible to pick up the faintest of residues. The machine was put to work on the obvious pieces of evidence—the ransom note, the duct tape, the wooden ligature handle, the floor where JonBenét's body was found, and likely candidates for the blunt instrument which had been used to fracture JonBenét's skull.

Still, police refused to comment on substantive questions, such as the time of JonBenét's death, whether she was dead before reaching the basement, and how she might have gotten to the basement without anyone else in the house hearing anything.

Boulder police chief Koby told the *Daily Camera* that he wouldn't answer any of those questions.

"The public," Koby said, "doesn't need to

know. They want to know." In Koby's view, there
was an important difference between needing to
know and wanting to know, one often blurred
by both the news media and officials responding
to public pressures.

The following day, however, another detail
about the crime leaked out. The ransom note, it
appeared, had been written on a yellow legal
pad. The pad itself had been found in the Ramsey house during the police search. That, the
Post suggested, meant that JonBenét's killer
hadn't brought the ransom note into the house
before the contact with JonBenét, but had written it there.

The note, indeed, was peculiar. Two-and-a-
half pages is considered extremely long for a
ransom note. The lettering was in block letters,
fashioned with a felt-tip pen. In addition to the
unusual ransom demand—for the oddly specific amount of $118,000—there were the ref-
erences to John's naval career at "SBTC," and
references to John's business dealings.

It was possible that the killer had brought the
legal pad into the house as he or she entered,
but it wasn't very likely. Why bring the entire
pad, rather than just the note? Why leave it behind? It seemed more reasonable to assume
that the killer had found the pad in the house
and had then written the note.

But would a kidnapper do that? Why waste
time and subject himself to possible discovery
by writing a note while at the crime scene itself?

It didn't seem very likely. Instead, the greater probability was that the note was written *after* the murder as part of an attempt to cover up, or at least conceal for a time, the crime of murder. Given the evidence of sexual assault, it seemed far more likely that the motive for the crime was psychosexual in origin, and that, in the aftermath of the murder, the note was written as a blind.

And who could have composed such a note in the stressful aftermath of a murderous sexual assault? Who would have known where to find the legal pad? Who would have known the things about John Ramsey that were included in the text? Only, it appeared, someone who was familiar with the house, who was comfortable in the environment, who knew he or she wasn't likely to be discovered and was willing to take the time to write a lengthy note, to deposit it in the location were it was certain to be discovered before the body was found. The universe of possibilities was exceedingly small.

A HORRIBLE NIGHTMARE

Against the backdrop of leaks and speculation, John Ramsey began mounting his
own offensive. Acting on the recommendation of
his newly hired Denver lawyers, John employed
a Washington, D.C., public relations firm to
handle inquiries from the press and respond to
developments in the case. The so-called "Ramsey Team" began to take shape.

The new Ramsey spokesman was Patrick Korten, a former radio journalist who had worked
as a spokesman for the U.S. Department of Justice under former Attorney General Ed Meese.
Korten's firm was Rowan & Blewitt, a public relations firm that billed itself as specialists in
"crisis management"—in other words, "spin
control."

In addition to Rowan & Blewitt, John's Denver
lawyer, Bryan Morgan, also retained a prominent Denver-area private investigator, H. Ellis

Armistead. Armistead, a former Lakewood, Colorado, police officer who had also worked as a district attorney's investigator, was said to have an excellent reputation in law enforcement and legal circles. Over the following week, a number of other experts would line up on the Ramsey side, including one of the nation's most prominent experts in criminal psychological profiling, former FBI Agent John Douglas. It appeared that John Ramsey was willing to spare no expense to clear away any suspicions and find the killer of his daughter.

On the Friday after the Ramseys had returned to Boulder—they had stayed with friends because, Nedra Paugh told a Denver television station, "Patsy will never go back to that hellhole," [the Ramsey house]—the Boulder police chief Tom Koby held a press conference to defend his department's actions in the case.

By this time, the influx of outside news media had begun to shoot pointed questions at the police, chief among them why the police had permitted John to find the body on his own when they apparently had a legal search warrant already in hand. Koby was also getting heat from a Denver *Post* columnist named Chuck Green, who suggested that the Boulder police had bungled the investigation from the beginning due primarily to their deference to John as a wealthy man and powerful employer in the community.

In a column titled "Class has its Privileges,"

Green asserted that the one place in America where class ought to have no privilege was in the "eye of the police and the law."

"Otherwise," wrote Green, "trust in government deteriorates, trust in each other decays, and the republic slowly rots.

"In Boulder this month," Green concluded, "that trust is being severely tested."

Koby was, like John Ramsey, a 1991 arrival in Boulder. He previously served as a ranking officer in Houston, Texas. In many ways, Koby seemed to fit the image of Boulder: rarely excitable, understated, community-oriented. No matter how many rocks Chuck Green threw at him, or the Ramsey team, or even CNN, Koby seemed determined to conduct the JonBenét investigation by the book—methodically, accurately, and regardless of the demands of the evening news.

"It's not O.J., and it's not L.A. here in Boulder," Koby said at his press conference on Friday, January 3. "Our guy won't walk. We are not going to be a part of a media circus. Our goal is to remain focused on apprehending the person or persons responsible for JonBenét Ramsey's death and getting a conviction."

Mayor Leslie Durgin had her own press conference, and like Koby's, it was televised lived by CNN.

"I've been asked if there is widespread fear in Boulder," Mayor Durgin said, "and the answer is no. There is no widespread fear in Boulder.

People in Boulder have no need to fear there is someone wandering the streets of Boulder looking for someone to attack. Boulder is safe. Boulder is a safe community, and it will continue to be."

The reason for the reticence, both Koby and Durgin said, wasn't to punish or repudiate the news media, but to keep information known only to the police and the killer confidential. Once secret details of the crime got into the public domain, the police would have a far harder time interrogating any eventual suspect.

But Koby's insistence that the police would continue to keep mum about details of the case began to fall apart at almost the same time that he was saying Boulder was not L.A., and the case wasn't like O.J.

In addition to the *Post*'s story about the nylon cord and the stick, a story appeared the same day in the *Rocky Mountain News*. Reporter Charlie Brennan disclosed that JonBenét's skull had been fractured with a blow to the head, and that the blow had come before the strangulation. Brennan had the detail about the nylon ligature and reported that JonBenét had been "sexually abused."

Brennan also reported a new fact: that investigators were struck by parallels between the ransom note found in the Ramsey house that seemed similar to a note left behind in the Mel Gibson movie, *Ransom*.

The warning to the Ramseys to prepare for a

difficult ordeal echoed the words used in the Gibson movie, in which Gibson was advised to prepare for a "rigorous" ordeal. Similarly, in *Ransom*, Gibson was both a pilot and a businessman; the movie victim's mouth was taped, and the movie ransom note began, "I have your son."

All of this raised the possibility that if the note was written after the murder, it was by someone who had seen the Gibson movie.

The media invasion of their lives ignited Nedra Paugh, Patsy's mother. In an interview published Sunday, January 5, in the *Daily Camera*, Nedra contended the news media was attempting to destroy John.

"We've lost our little girl," Nedra told *Camera* staff writer Alli Krupski, "and now the press is trying to destroy my son-in-law. I don't know why they're trying to do that."

The coverage, Nedra said, had infuriated the Ramseys' old friends in Atlanta. Particularly bothersome was the mob scene on her street earlier in the week.

"This is the first time the TV cameras haven't been outside," she said. "We want people to get down on their knees and pray to the Lord that He reveals the facts so that He can stop this horrible nightmare."

EVIDENCE

By the time Nedra had given her interview to the *Daily Camera*, the Boulder police had finally finished their exhaustive search of the Ramsey house. Reporters who had staked out the search scene kept track of officers' comings and goings for almost eight days. Two crime scene vans remained parked in front of the dwelling for most of the time while the search continued.

At one point, investigators wearing rubber gloves took the doorknobs off doors on either side of the house. New knobs were installed. At another point, a number of investigators went into a neighbor's house, stayed about ten minutes, then went back inside the Ramsey house. News people were unable to raise anyone at the neighbor's house to find out what was going on.

Late Saturday afternoon, January 4, several

deputy district attorneys were on the scene and held an animated discussion with searching officers. The media didn't know what that was about either.

Leslie Aaholm continued to try to set the press straight.

"There are certain facts in this case that only the killer and the police are aware of," she said, "and it is vital to our investigation that the integrity of the information remain intact. The likelihood of getting a successful conclusion to this case is based on maintaining the security of the information."

But by Monday there was a new leak, this time to the *Daily Camera*, which reported for the first time, rather off-handedly, that police had collected samples of "bodily fluid" from the area where JonBenét's body had been discovered.

In ensuing days, as the "bodily fluid" was discussed, hashed and rehashed in the news media, it slowly came to be assumed that the fluid was semen. Experts in forensic analysis explained about DNA analysis, and cited semen testing as an example. Somehow, without anyone officially confirming the fact, the idea took root that the critical sample *was* semen. In fact, it could have been saliva or blood, all of which contain DNA, and any one of which can be compared to any other to see whether the DNA matches. In other words, a sample of DNA from a blood sample can be compared to DNA from a semen or saliva sample because DNA is very nearly unique and is the same regardless of what kind of biological form it originated in.

And regardless of the origin of any such sample, the same principles of forensic science apply. The searching officer who locates the sample—in some cases the sample is recovered during an autopsy, in others it may be obvious to the naked eye in the environment, or in still others it may be present in very small, hard-to-detect amounts—is required to collect it carefully and preserve it. If the amount is extremely small, it may be detected by such a device as the Omniprint laser detector.

Obviously, the likeliest place to look for such samples, besides JonBenét's body, was where John had discovered her in the wine cellar; JonBenét's bedroom; the place near the Christmas tree where John had put her body after bringing her from the basement; and possibly the stairs, since presumably the killer had used stairs to take JonBenét from her bedroom to the basement.

But in a fifteen-room house, there were other possibilities as well. A thorough investigation required that each room be examined for possible "bodily fluid" evidence and other biological evidence susceptible to forensic analysis such as hairs, skin, fingernails, or feces. That was one reason the search took so long: to leave no corner of the sprawling house unexamined.

Once the questioned samples—the evidence—

were collected, they were taken to the Colorado
Bureau of Investigation's crime laboratory,
where, presumably, they were properly inven-
toried and preserved. The next step would be to
extract the DNA from the evidence and subject
part of it to a special process in which the DNA
in essence is "grown" to increase the sample
size. At that point the DNA is examined to determine the "alleles"—or chromosomal pattern—
of the DNA donor. Then the alleles from the control sample—such as those taken from the
Ramseys and their friends—are compared to
those from the evidence. If the chromosomal
makeup matches, the odds are overwhelming
that the person who left the evidence sample is
the same as the person who was tested.

Or so the theory goes. So far, DNA evidence
has been both widely hailed by forensic scien-
tists and condemned by some lawyers. Most
courts have so far accepted DNA evidence and
its various means of testing as information that
can be put before a jury, for a jury to decide as
to its value.

But, as the nation saw in the Simpson case,
the mere presence of DNA at a crime scene is
not necessarily proof of guilt—and it might especially not be proof of guilt in a dwelling unit
frequented by one of the people whose sample
matches. There could be many explanations for
how biological material may have arrived at any
given point, and many of them may be benign.
Obviously, the more closely associated with the

victim the evidence sample is, the more the likelihood is that the sample may have been involved in the crime.

Besides the biological evidence, there are other kinds of trace evidence to be considered—fibers, for example. A person wearing a certain type of clothing may leave fibers on or near the victim. Those fibers must be handled very carefully, with complete documentation of every step back to their initial discovery. Often, forensic experts use a combination of magnifying glass and transparent tape to look for and collect these fibers, many of which may be minute. Each fiber must be catalogued as to its origin, and if possible identified. Sometimes a fiber can be identified as coming from a specific piece of clothing; that too would be considered acceptable evidence against a perpetrator in a trial. As a result, garments worn by possible suspects are often collected by police and similarly inspected. Samples taken by transparent tape from these control garments are then compared to the questioned fibers from the evidence.

Much the same is true with hair. People are continually shedding hair of various kinds. Sex crimes in particular yield abundant hair evidence. Often, if the hair is not visible to the naked eye—frequently it is not—at some point an officer with a powerful vacuum cleaner will scour the evidentiary surface, such as a carpet, to pick up every hair that is in the area. Not infrequently a large section of carpet from the

crime scene is cut up and removed so that the
vacuuming can be done under controlled conditions. Also picked up are specks of soil, sometimes paint flakes, tiny bits of broken glass that
may have come from another surface—indeed,
the potential points of origin for such "trace evidence," as it's called, are legion. Each piece of
trace evidence can tell a forensic investigator a
potentially crucial tale.

If, for example, a tiny bit of broken glass found
at a crime scene matches identical glass taken
from a room in which a suspect has been known
to have occupied, it would be suggestive that the
occupant of the room had been in both places
at some point in the past.

Or, in another case, a hair found in one location might be compared to a hair found in a
second location; both hairs in turn might be
compared to a known sample from a suspect. If
the hairs are all the same kind of hair in terms
of color, structure, and size, it would be suggestive that the suspect had been in both places.

This sort of painstaking evidence collection
takes many hours and requires a great deal of
thoroughness; it was exactly what had been going on in the Ramsey house for the better part
of eight days.

Thus, by late Saturday night, when the Boulder police finally took down the yellow crime-
scene tape that had surrounded the Ramsey
house for so long—and had begun to unnerve
the neighbors—the most critical evidence in the

case was on its way to the Colorado Bureau of Investigation. It would be up to the CBI to put together the puzzle of what happened to Jon-Benét Ramsey.

HALF FULL

——

On Sunday, after the Boulder police had vacated the Ramsey house, the Ramsey Team got its first crack at the scene. Private investigators hired by Bryan Morgan, Ramsey's Denver lawyer, entered the house to familiarize themselves with the layout and begin hazarding guesses as to what the official detectives had removed.

Meanwhile, the Ramseys and the police seemed to be engaging in a struggle of maneuver over when and where the police might conduct a formal interview. It was reported that not only were the Boulder police surprised that the Ramseys gave an interview to CNN, they were also angered. No police investigator feels comfortable with watching the news media conduct an interview that more appropriately ought be conducted first by the official authorities. Some detectives began to suspect that the Ramseys were making an end-run around the authorities, a feeling that was bolstered by the Ramseys' hiring of lawyers, private investigators, and spin doctors.

At least part of the problem, in retrospect, appears to have stemmed from Boulder city officials' insistence that the murder was no random, stranger-to-stranger killing. While this might have been justified in order to avert a panic in Boulder—or even maintain Boulder's image—it nevertheless had the effect of focusing suspicion directly on the Ramsey family. Under such circumstances it was hardly surprising that a man with means would take steps to protect himself, even if that included declining to consent to a formal interview.

Patrick Korten, the Ramsey "media consultant," told reporters on Sunday that the Ramsey Team had begun "working with" the Boulder police, although that seems to have been more in anticipation than in fact. After all, the Ramsey Team had only gained access to the murder scene that day. The Boulder police had given the Ramseys a list of written questions to answer, Korten added, and the Ramseys had complied.

When asked by the *Post*, however, why no formal interview by the police had yet taken place, Korten responded, "legal prudence," and added, "In a case where your clients may be considered suspects, however unlikely, your job as a lawyer is to manage very carefully the time, manner, and methods of your cooperation with the police."

By that time it had also been learned that a separate lawyer, Patrick Burke, had been retained for Patsy Ramsey.

Meanwhile, the usual media crowd staked out the Ramseys' Boulder church, St. John's Episcopal, hoping for a shot of the bereaved suspects and as likely, a chance to shout out a question designed to elicit some visceral reaction. Korten arranged a "photo op" to take place after the services so the media could get images of the Ramseys leaving church. Korten said he did this to avoid turning the service into a "media circus."

Submitting written questions to principal witnesses in a homicide case is unusual but not unheard of, particularly when there are difficulties arranging a formal interview. In the case of the Ramseys, the investigators had an entire series of what they termed "housekeeping questions" that were necessary to develop any leads in the case. But police still wanted a formal interview, Boulder County Assistant District Attorney Bill Wise told the *Rocky Mountain News*.

"To do otherwise," Wise said, "would not be treating them as they treat other suspects. A real interview that goes to the heart of the matter must take place and must take place in a police setting."

The written questions, Wise said, involved

who else might have had access to the Ramsey house, such as milk deliverers, recent package deliveries, the names of handymen who might have worked around the house, and the like.

Beyond these, Wise said, the district attorney's office had advised the police that no more written questions were to be propounded to the Ramseys.

On the Monday following the Ramseys' appearance at St. John's, it was learned that a team of Boulder detectives had gone to Charlevoix, Michigan, obtained a local search warrant, and searched the Ramsey vacation home there over the weekend.

Boulder police declined to comment on why they wanted to search the Ramsey vacation home, but Boulder police chief Tom Koby offered a cryptic hint in responding to questions at what was billed as a "routine" press briefing.

"There is a tendency," Koby said, "to see the glass half empty. But we continue to investigate all possibilities, including the possibility of a kidnapping. We have not eliminated anything or anyone. To read between the lines on this is to do exactly that. A lot of times, there's nothing there."

What did this mean?

A parsing of Koby's remarks seemed to indicate that Boulder police had theorized that perhaps there might be evidence in the Charlevoix vacation house that might tie that circle of Ramsey acquaintances to a possible kidnapping attempt. And further, Koby seemed to be suggesting that leaping to the conclusion that the Ramseys might be involved in the death of their daughter was to see the glass as half-empty, rather than the whole glass itself.

But the Ramseys' apparent reluctance to sit down with the police in a formal interview continued to gnaw at the press, which quickly dug up experts to criticize the police for their failure to insist on an immediate interview.

"I have never heard of a homicide investigation being done that way," an unnamed man billed as a "high-ranking police official in the metro area" told the *Post*.

Others were equally astounded. California father Mark Klass, whose daughter Polly was kidnapped and murdered in northern California several years earlier, made an appearance on a Philadelphia, Pennsylvania morning show, *AM Live* on WPVI, an ABC affiliate. The fact that JonBenét's murder had become a national topic was clearly apparent in the Philadelphia station's choice of subject matter.

"I think," Mark Klass told the broadcaster, "that the parents have made some terrible decisions thus far by hiring lawyers and a publicist and refusing to talk to police. And instead they go to CNN. They put themselves in a very defensive mode. I think it does not serve them well at all to put themselves in that kind of a position."

Of course, there were significant differences between Klass's position and the situation of the Ramseys: Klass was not in his house when his daughter was kidnapped and murdered and thus had an ironclad alibi.

Still, Klass suggested that the Ramseys submit to a lie detector test.

"You get on the polygraph," he said, "and you do whatever you have to do to move suspicion away from yourself so that law enforcement can focus all their resources on the other options that exist."

Left once more without anything new to report, the media crowd put on its detective hat once more and began scouring the Charlevoix area for new leads. The *News* discovered the Ramseys' Charlevoix telephone number and dialed it. The voice that came on the line was that of JonBenét Ramsey.

"We're having a great summer," JonBenét's recorded voice said. "Wish you were here."

MORE LEAKS

O n the following day, Wednesday, it was reported that Chief of Police Tom Koby had
moved to plug leaks in his department. It was
announced that Sergeant Larry Mason had
been removed from the case as lead investigator.

A city spokesman put out a formal statement.

"Boulder police chief Tom Koby has removed
Detective Sgt. Larry Mason from the Ramsey
homicide investigation effective Sunday, January 5. In doing so, the police chief explained that
when this investigation began, the mission
would be a very focused one: finding out who is
responsible and securing a conviction.

"All other issues, including intense media
scrutiny, will not be allowed to deter the Boulder
Police Department from its singular focus. The
chief has made it clear that anyone distracted
from this focus will be reassigned.

"Due to a rule governing personnel actions, we are limited in what we can say about this matter. Boulder police continue to have ample resources dedicated to this investigation."

This appeared to suggest that Mason had somehow become "distracted" from the "focus" and also that Mason wasn't happy about the abrupt transfer.

Despite Mason's removal—or perhaps as a result of it—there was yet another leak from the Boulder police investigation that had appeared in the papers that same morning. "Sources" told the *Daily Camera*, the *Post*, and the *Rocky Mountain News* that detectives had discovered what appeared to be a "practice" ransom note in the Ramsey house.

A practice ransom note? That clearly seemed to indicate that the note was written after the murder. What kidnapper would bring his practice note along with him or her when going to abduct the victim?

All the newspapers reported that the so-called practice note had been written on the same pad of legal paper that had been associated with the real note. The idea seemed to be that after having committed the murder, the killer sat down to figure out what to do next and struck upon the idea of writing a kidnapping ransom note to explain JonBenét's disappearance. Unsatisfied with the first attempt, the killer started over.

The sources told the newspapers that the

block handwriting was "shaky" at the beginning of the practice note. The *News* reported that some sources believed that the killer had attempted to disguise the handwriting in the beginning but smoothed it out as the flow of words began to take form.

The note itself was beginning to assume larger and larger evidentiary value. The investigators had already taken handwriting samples from the Ramseys, some of their employees, employees of Access Graphics, and friends of the family. The idea was to subject the ransom notes to handwriting comparisons to see whether a match might be found.

Despite fictional canards in which it's possible to disguise handwriting, it is in actuality quite a difficult task to accomplish—particularly the longer a writing sample is. Two different notes aggregating nearly three pages is an enormously large sample of writing.

Analysis of such writing is more than just comparisons of the letters themselves. Almost as important—in some cases even more important—is an evaluation of the way the letters are formed. Strokes and pressure for various letters are the key, even if the letters are dissimilar. Crossing a T in a certain manner, such as a longer, downward sloping stroke can be a meaningful piece of evidence, particularly if such an example occurs rather later in the recovered sample, when presumably the writer is writing faster and therefore more naturally.

Additionally, the recovery of two different ransom notes—possibly from different areas of the house—was a clear indication of the killer's movements on the night of the murder.

And while no one was talking about it, the possibility existed that fingerprints might exist on the two notes. Clearly John and Patsy's prints were on at least one note, the first one; but what if one or the other's prints were on the second note? Indeed, what if a third person's prints were on both notes?

Finally, the wording of the two notes was itself evidence. The psychological clues present in the wording were a window into the personality of the killer. Already police had noted the similarity between the words of the first ransom note and the note in the Mel Gibson movie, *Ransom.* Were there other clues as well? Was, for example, the reference to SBTC psychologically significant, perhaps showing a connection between John Ramsey and the perpetrator? Was there evidence of apology in the note? Or regret? Either of these might be consistent with a killer who had killed on impulse and shortly after has devised some sort of excuse and explanation, however bizarre and untrue. Reading deeper into the note might suggest something of the psychological relationship between the Ramseys and the killer. That was one reason why the police were unconvinced that the killer had been the act of a random stranger.

All of which made it imperative for the police

to have the long-awaited formal interview with the Ramseys: to probe, gently if possible, harder if necessary, these potential psychologically loaded possibilities.

The first notes had already been packed off to the Colorado Bureau of Investigation for handwriting analysis. The FBI would also take a look at the wording in an effort to develop a psychological profile of the killer, based upon his or her own words.

So, too, would the Ramsey Team. The Ramseys' lawyers wanted the police to let their experts look at the notes as well. At length, after consideration, the police gave the Ramsey Team a copy of the notes. The Ramsey lawyers hired their own handwriting experts, who began to set about their own analysis.

Very soon thereafter, *Newsweek* reported that the Ramsey experts had concluded that neither Patsy nor John had written the notes.

MEDIA MADNESS

D etective Sergeant Mason's banishment from the investigation had no apparent effect on the leaks, which continued to seep out. Whether the leaks were coming from Mason himself, other detectives, the district attorney's office, or Team Ramsey's spin control operation wasn't clear. But it was soon learned that the ransom had been demanded in $100 bills, that a bank in Boulder had put the sum together early in the morning of the day the murder was discovered, and that the blunt instrument that had crushed JonBenét's skull was consistent with a baseball bat or perhaps a pipe.

"It just really smashed the side of her head," a source told the *Daily Camera*.

The papers also reported that the Colorado Bureau of Investigation hadn't completed its own analysis of the writing in the notes, and that no final conclusions as to the author had been drawn. That appeared to fall somewhat short of the Ramsey team's conclusions that neither Patsy nor John had been the writer.

Criticism of the Boulder Police Department was continuing and growing more pointed.

In the question-mark headline style favored by the Denver *Post*, the paper asked, "Did Boulder cops stumble at start?"

In a story by staff writers Mark Eddy and Marilyn Robinson, the paper noted that standard police procedure in a kidnapping case was to seal the crime scene.

While true, it was likewise that, at the time the police first responded to the Ramsey house, no one knew where the crime scene was, except, perhaps the stairs where the note was found, or JonBenét's bedroom.

All of this came back to the confusion over who did what on the morning of the kidnapping. By this point, various scenarios had moved into the public arena: John's assertion that police had searched the house that morning but had failed to find anything; the reported police assertion that John had refused to give formal permission to search; and the actual event, in which Boulder police officers and assistant district attorneys, armed with a legal warrant received about noon and delivered to the house around one P.M., simply sat around for at least a half-hour, doing nothing, before a police suggestion was made that John himself search the house.

This last clearly was not acceptable police procedure. The *Post* found a police expert to say exactly why:

"Normally," said Patrick Furman, a criminology professor at the University of Colorado, "I would expect the police to conduct that search. There may be good reasons why the normal police procedure wasn't followed, but I would expect them to do it. They're trained in this sort of thing and the normal citizen is not."

Another expert, identified as Tony Palmer of International Law Enforcement and Consulting of Walnut Creek, California, observed that, at the very least, an officer should have accompanied John during the search. Palmer suggested that John's discovery and removal of the body had "ruined" the crime scene. It wasn't John's fault, Palmer said, but the police could have prevented it.

And given the fact that the police had in hand the warrant that gave them the power to search, the fact that no officer accompanied John seems inexplicable, even if, at that early point, police were suspicious of John. Certainly, if they *had* been suspicious of John and suggested the search in order to give him a chance to "discover" the body, correct procedure should have been to have an officer accompany him to observe his actions and reactions. The fact that the police had a warrant at the time, which would have empowered them to accompany him, makes this particularly disturbing.

As for an immediate and thorough search of the crime scene, the *Post* quoted a former head of the Denver FBI office, Bob Pence, saying that in kidnapping situations, the Bureau likes to conduct "an exhaustive search of the immediate premises . . . because that is the crime scene."

Just why the FBI agents from Boulder and Denver arriving at the house on the morning of the kidnapping report didn't do just that was also unclear.

Meanwhile, Charlie Brennan of the *Rocky Mountain News* continued to pump his unnamed sources for further details about the lamentably unsearched crime scene. Brennan reported that the door to the wine cellar had been stuck shut, and that was one reason why police did not go into the room when they first arrived on the scene.

As for JonBenét's body and the position it was found in—as noted, critical evidence about the possible state of mind of the killer immediately after the murder—Brennan's sources told him that JonBenét's arms were flung back over her head, which seemed to suggest that the killer had left her lying on her back. Brennan's sources noted, moreover, that the cord tied around JonBenét's left wrist matched the fiber in the cord found around her neck, but that it left no abrasions on her wrist. That suggested to investigators, Brennan reported, that the cord had been tied to the wrist after the murder had occurred.

That afternoon, by the sort of weird alchemy that so often attends such high-profile murder cases, rumors swept through the media that the police had obtained a confession from John Ramsey. Reporters turned the town upside town seeking confirmation and a reaction, again flooding the Ramseys' neighborhood with reporters, and even going to John Andrew's fraternity house at the university to see if it was true. One reporter even sneaked into the back of the frat house in an attempt to find out what was going on, only to be discovered and bodily ejected.

The rumors, of course, were untrue; and afterward, no one seemed to be able to explain how they started or where they had come from.

That night, in the face of the growing criticism of his department, Tom Koby conducted a sort of televised community roundtable on the case, in which questions would be asked by reporters. The chief's most severe critics, including the *Post's* Eddy and Robinson, and the *News'* Brennan and Green, were not included.

Chief Koby began the program by reading from a prepared statement.

"Two weeks ago today," Koby said, "a violent criminal act took away from this community one of our innocents, JonBenét Ramsey. She did not deserve to be killed, for she had done nothing in her young life to harm anyone.

"We are grieving as a community for our loss.

I hope to use this forum as a means to aid that process. I hope to provide insight into this event that has been difficult to communicate because of the inherent conflict between the media's desire to provide all of the information they can obtain and the Boulder Police Department's desire to protect the integrity of our investigation.

"I have had many members of this community ask me about comments indicating that there is a killer loose in our community. The question this raises: is there a need for community members to be fearful?

"There is no question," Koby continued, "that there is a person or persons responsible for this act who have not been apprehended. It is my advice now, as it is at any time, that we need to be vigilant with respect to persons who may do harm to us. But this needs to be kept in perspective. In this country in the last two years, sixty-five percent of the homicides have been cleared. That means that in thirty-five percent of the cases of murder in the United States, the person responsible has not been apprehended. The reality we all live with every day is that we have many dangerous people in this community and communities across the country who are walking the streets.

"We all know this intellectually," Koby said. "However, we really never have to deal with it until it strikes close to us. We were not living in fear before this incident, and we cannot be forced to live in fear now.

"It is the best judgment of the Boulder Police Department that this is a one-time occurrence. The killing of JonBenét does not appear to be linked to any other similar event. What this means is that we do not believe we have a serial situation to deal with. Should the Boulder community be concerned and vigilant? Yes. Should we be living in fear? No. Can I guarantee this won't happen again? No."

Koby continued:

"There have been many stories and much speculation about who killed JonBenét. This is an area that I know will be explored in greater detail in the questions to follow. Let me offer a perspective on this issue. Prejudging and media hype have never solved a crime. Crime solving requires diligent and careful police work, and that is exactly what the Boulder Police Department is committed to doing.

"It is a natural response to a tragedy like this for the community to want to know immediately who is responsible. It is often an effort to assure ourselves that such a tragedy will never happen to us. The reality of the situation is that often these types of investigations may take time to solve.

"The integrity and competence of the men and women of the Boulder Police Department have been challenged. Let me first say that I have never had the privilege with working with more competent, dedicated professionals. They are getting the job done. We will not lose the focus of this investigation to respond to meaningless and unfounded remarks. This organization is well respected in our community. That respect has been earned over many years because of the level of competent service we have provided. Again, it is unfortunate to offer criticism which has no basis in fact.

"Let me assure the citizens of Boulder that the men and women of this department are doing everything that can be done to solve this case. All of our resources that my people have needed to do their work have been provided. Our success is very good in homicide investigations. Over the last five years, 1990 to 1995, we have had fifteen homicides in Boulder. We have solved thirteen of them. That means we have an eight-five percent rate of success with these investigations.

"We are not working on this investigation alone. When we have needed assistance, we have reached out to those who could provide help. Alex Hunter, the district attorney, has had his personnel working with us from the first hours of this investigation. George Epp, Boulder County sheriff, has provided us support in the areas of crime scene search and interviewing of witnesses. Pat Alstrom, director of the Colorado Department of Public Safety, has the Colorado Bureau of Investigations processing the evidence we have submitted as quickly and effectively as possible. The Federal Bureau of Investigation, Denver and Boulder offices, has provided us its expertise as we have asked for it.

"This violent act has deeply affected the members of the Boulder Police Department. We are fortunate that we work in an environment where we have not built up the hardened shell which you often find in other communities. But that means we still feel for the victims of violent crime. We are vulnerable. Many of us are parents who have felt this loss very deeply. We are doing our own debriefings within the organization to deal with our grief just as the community members are participating in debriefings to help themselves cope. The support we have received from the community means a great deal to us. Thank you."

Koby went on to thank the city's officials, including Mayor Durgin, for their support. Then he went on:

"Last, before we get into the questioning: let me be very clear about the focus of the Boulder Police Department in this matter. Our allegiance is solely to JonBenét Ramsey. We have a mission. We have dedicated ourselves to bringing to justice the person or persons responsible for her death. Everything else is secondary. We will not be deterred."

After this, Koby began fielding questions.

When pressed about the events of the morning when the kidnapping was reported and the failure to conduct a thorough search, Koby said, "I think what people have a hard time under-

standing is what was going on. You have to understand that what the Boulder Police Department was originally called to respond to was a
kidnapping, an in-process kidnapping."

There was, Koby said, a "preliminary search"
of the house. "And remember," he added, "this
is a very big house, it took us eight days to work
through this house." The preliminary search,
Koby said, was only to determine if there was
anything obvious that officers "needed to pay attention to."

It wasn't true, as had been reported, Koby
said, that the evidence in the house had been
compromised by John's discovery and removal
of the body.

Koby was asked whether his department
would have treated the case differently if the
family involved had been anyone other than a
wealthy business executive and a child beauty
queen. Koby counterattacked, calling the media's constant prodding and probing an "assault."

"It is something," he said, "that means a great
deal to the Boulder community, and that's why
we're here tonight. This situation is a curiosity
to the rest of the country—and quite frankly, it
is a sick curiosity.

"Why has the media given so much attention
to this case?" Koby asked. "If you and your colleagues want to help us, back off a little bit and
give us room to do our jobs."

The fact that the Ramseys hired legal counsel

was completely appropriate, Koby said, and had led to speculation that was "totally unfair."

"There has been nothing done by us or the Ramseys that is out of order."

When he was asked about officers' conversations with John and Patsy the morning of the reported kidnapping, Koby said that while they were "communicating" with John and Patsy, it wasn't the same as "interviewing" them. An interview, Koby said, "would have been totally unreasonable at that point in time"—meaning, before the discovery of the body, when everyone believed that a kidnapping had occurred.

Koby was pressed for confirmation of the details of the death as had recently been reported in the newspapers. But Koby refused to respond to those questions with any confirmation.

"One of the difficulties we're dealing with is the desire for great detail that is media interest but has a negative impact on our ability to solve the case," he said.

But if Koby believed that the media's interest in the murder had had a negative impact so far, he hadn't seen anything yet. The following day, in fact, Koby learned for the first time that secret crime scene photographs of JonBenét's dead body had been leaked to one of the supermarket tabloids, and that the photographs were about to be published for the whole world to see.

OVER THE LINE

The word about the *Globe*, a $1.39-a-week supermarket tabloid based in Boca Raton, Florida, had come to Boulder County Coroner John Meyer from the NBC bureau chief in Denver, Jack Chestnut. Chestnut told the *Daily Camera* that his staff had received an advance copy of the forthcoming January 21 edition of the paper, which had a usual circulation of 1.3 million copies a week. Five photos of the crime scene, including a fairly gruesome close-up shot of the nylon ligature and the stick used to twist it—still entangled with JonBenét's hair—were featured in the *Globe's* story on the murder.

"Our interest in the photos were (sic) on two levels," NBC's Chestnut explained to the *Daily Camera.* "One, were they authentic? And two, had they been taken from the coroner's office? We were never interested in putting the *Globe's* photos on the air, and we will not broadcast them."

After hearing about the photos from Chestnut, Meyer called the offices of district attorney Alex Hunter and Boulder County sheriff George Epp. Then he did something he knew he would have to do, however unpleasant: he called the lawyers representing the Ramseys to let them know what had happened, so they might be prepared for yet another shock. Meyer apparently saw the advance copy of the tabloid, because he quickly determined that the photos were genuine, taken at either the crime scene or the coroner's office.

Epp immediately assigned three deputies to find out how the tabloid had gained possession of the photographs. Law enforcement officials roundly condemned the *Globe*'s decision to publish the apparently purloined pictures as "sick."

The *Post* tracked down the *Globe*'s editor, Tony Frost, to ask him what was going on. Frost defended the use of the photographs.

"These photos are the essence of the case," Frost said. "They say it all." Frost also said his paper would cooperate with Sheriff Epps's investigation but would do nothing to compromise their sources, a sort of double-talk, since the essence of Epps's investigation was to find out who the *Globe*'s sources were.

Again the problem of maintaining the confidentiality of the investigators' information was raised. Because the photographs showed specific information, primarily about the ligature, the stick, and the cord around JonBenét's wrists, these facts could no longer be used by investigators to goad a potential suspect into an incriminating admission. A suspect, for example, could simply say that he or she had seen the *Globe* photos, and that was how he or she knew the details of the death scene.

After almost three weeks of siege by reporters and camera crews from all over the country, the *Globe's* action was, for many in Boulder, the last straw. The means of expression of public distaste were different than in Roswell, where residents had confronted reporters by calling them "vultures" to their faces. In progressive Boulder, a boycott of the tabloid was organized. This in turn touched off a typically Boulder dispute between those who said the supermarkets shouldn't offer the tabloid for sale and those who said the boycott amounted to censorship. Safeway stores quickly dispatched clerks to snatch up copies of the tabloid at checkout stands all across the nation, while in Denver, the owner of a newsstand defiantly offered the *Globe* for free. The publisher of an east Boulder County weekly stuffed his paper with free copies of the *Globe* as a protest of the boycott.

Meanwhile, the Ramseys' media consultant, Patrick Korten, issued a statement on the *Globe's* decision to use the crime scene photographs. By this point, Korten's employer, Rowan & Blewitt, had established an Internet website for information about the case. The written statement was posted on the site—probably the first time in history the family of a murder victim had used such technology to get its side of the story out.

"The ghoulish publication of these photographs by the *Globe* is beneath contempt," Korten's statement said. "It is a callous act that poses a grave threat to the integrity of the criminal investigation of JonBenét's murder and has caused unimaginable pain to the family. In publishing these photos, the editors of the *Globe* have shown themselves to be jackals, not journalists. We call upon all other media to decline to republish or televise these photos out of consideration for the Ramsey family. Our attorneys have been directed to pursue all available avenues of legal recourse."

Beneath the uproar over the photos was another issue: just why had the *Globe* done such a thing, and what had they hoped to accomplish? One had to read the *Globe* article to fathom that. It turned out that the *Globe* had given copies of the photographs it obtained to a noted forensic pathologist, Dr. Cyril Wecht, of Pittsburgh, Pennsylvania. The *Globe* said Wecht—who once critiqued the autopsy of President John F. Kennedy—looked over the photographs and guessed that the ropes and ligature were used in a "sex game" that had suddenly turned fatal.

Wecht pointed to the fact that the cord on

JonBenét's wrists was tied around the outside of her clothing. He suggested that the killer had done this to avoid leaving any marks.

"When you bind someone in a sex game," the *Globe* quoted Wecht as saying, "you don't want to leave embarrassing marks that people might ask about."

Wecht, according to the *Globe*, further suggested that JonBenét's killer may have been someone known to her. The tabloid said Wecht did not believe that the motive for the crime was kidnapping but that the kidnapping idea was an afterthought once the supposed sex game had turned deadly.

A few nights later the uproar over the *Globe* photos was taken up by CNN's Larry King. He decided to explore the ethical issues raised by the *Globe's* action. He lassoed Frost and a lawyer for the tabloid, and put them into a televised rountable discussion with three reporters in Denver: Charlie Brennan from the *Rocky Mountain News*, a Denver television reporter, and a writer for a national magazine.

Was it proper for the *Globe* to have published the photographs? Frost and his lawyer insisted that it was. It wasn't just the photos, Frost said; the real question was what the photos showed about the psychological makeup of JonBenét's killer. Frost put Wecht out front, saying that the photos had been used by the paper to acquaint Dr. Wecht with information about the crime and the killer. That in turn came to the question of whether a "killer was on the loose" or if the murderer was someone known to the child. That was an advancement of the story, Frost contended, and in the finest traditions of American journalism.

King pitched the question to the reporters in Denver. Would they have published or broadcast the photos? All three said they would not have done so; it was perhaps an easy decision since they never had the chance to make the choice. All three also agreed that publishing the photographs did little to advance the story, and anyway, was in bad taste.

Bad taste. Here came the imponderable question at last: at what point does coverage of a sensational murder case cross the line from aggressive reporting to bad taste? The three reporters in Denver grappled with the question, but never were able to come to any clear definition of where the line might be. Instead, one launched into a discussion of the propriety of paying for information, as the *Globe* had apparently done. That wasn't proper, the journalists agreed, although that had less to do with taste than tactics. Frost said everyone knew the *Globe* and other supermarket tabloids paid cash for stories and photographs, so what was the big deal?

One of the real issues left on the table in King's round-robin discussion was how, at least in the public mind, the act of one journalist is the act of all. The *Globe's* use of the photographs, apparently obtained surreptitiously, could be seen as having brought discredit on the motives of all journalists and consequently making it all the more difficult for ethical reporters to do their jobs. A resistance to inquiry was sure to set in; and with Epp's investigators in pursuit of the photo leakers, a chill among sources was almost certain to develop as well.

That in turn made it far harder for the mainstream media to distinguish between fact and rumor, the first job of a reporter, and the blurring of which is the supermarket tabloids' stock-in-trade.

Still, the publicity from the *Globe's* action further stimulated public interest in JonBenét's murder; and it was hardly surprising that other supermarket tabloids raced to catch up. Soon the *Star,* the *National Enquirer,* and others had their own stories on the murder, largely based on blind quotes attributed to Ramsey family friends, which were completely unverifiable and often outlandish. At one point one tabloid quoted a former housekeeper for the Ramseys claiming that Patsy had complained to her about her sex life, which in some minds was an even more nauseating invasion of privacy than the *Globe's* photos.

By early the following week, the media frenzy had grown even more intense, probably in part due to the publication of the *Globe* pictures. The *Washington Post* dispatched two writers to Boulder, and CNN's contingent numbered somewhere around twenty bodies. *People* magazine had an even dozen in town. A desk clerk at a Boulder hotel said she'd heard estimates that as many as three hundred journalists were in the small town, waiting for something to happen.

A resident of the fraternity claiming John Andrew as one of its members told the *Denver Post* that relay teams of television crews had come to the frat house for interviews, only to be chased away by the brothers.

Some of the fraternity brothers called the reporters "leeches" or "sharks" and observed that they seemed to be running around in circles. The *Post* quoted one fraternity brother they identified as Josh Uebelherr recounting an experience he had with an NBC crew.

"Here's the weirdest," Uebelherr told the *Post*. "I was in the house a couple of days ago and some guy from NBC comes up to the door and asks me if the rumor someone confessed is true. Jeez, get some facts, guy."

Just why the NBC reporter, if indeed that was who he represented, thought that a presumably ignorant fraternity boy would have any real information as to whether a confession had been made seems, in retrospect, ridiculous. But in the absense of information, and under extreme competitive pressures and pressures from producers, directors, and editors, reporters will often do anything in preference to doing nothing.

Soon even reporters were criticizing one another for excesses, as were their employers.

The *Daily Camera* on the Monday following the *Globe* uproar fairly sneered with disgust in an editorial titled, "News that isn't Fit to Print" and jumped squarely with both feet on the ethics of the *Globe*.

"There is no way to prevent its [the *Globe's*] publication in a free society," the *Daily Camera* sniffed, "but there are at least three ways to reject it as the sick and poisonous thing it is." The three ways: don't buy it, don't read it, and tell anyone trying to sell it that they shouldn't.

The paper went on to observe that the legitimate role of the press is to provide timely information to the public and to "monitor the work of the police."

"Many in the public," the *Daily Camera* editorial continued, "are uneasy with the tone and extent of the coverage and will argue that the media have drawn the line in the wrong place."

The import of the *Daily Camera's* editorial was to suggest that it was up to the news media to enforce its own discipline; in other words, that the appropriate line between cashing in and expostulating was a matter of moral judgment; excesses that drove news coverage into tasteless and destructive revelations of both facts and insinuations could only be met by a self-imposed discipline that everyone longed for but didn't know how to impose. Editors and producers who knew better should take action to draw this line quite clearly, the *Camera* implied.

But this was something like asking a junkie to forswear his drug; shock and schlock sold the product, however slapped together and however erroneous. To pontificate from a one-newspaper town in which profits were assured, while simultaneously allowing reporters to run roughshod over the sensibilities of the Ramseys in the claimed interest of the public's right to know, ultimately smacked of hypocrisy.

While the *Camera*, or for that matter the *Washington Post* or *Los Angeles Times* or even the *New York Times*, fed on the media frenzy stoked by those publications' perception of the public's vicarious *desire* to know—Tom Koby's distinction between what the public needed and what it wanted—it only illustrated that the boundary line between reporting the news and taking advantage of the news was flexible indeed.

To the *Camera*, the *Globe* had gone too far; by its actions the *Globe* had denied that there was any line at all. That, the *Daily Camera* said, would never do.

To which, added others, amen; proving that the abuse of the mob was only a matter of degree, not intent.

DOUGLAS

By Monday, January 13, Sheriff George Epp was hot on the trail of the photo leakers. All the members of Dr. Meyer's coroner staff were "put on the box," or, as the phrase has it, given lie detector tests. So also were employees of the Boulder photoprocessing company that handled the coroner's film.

Meanwhile, Boulder County went to court to prevent the *Globe* from printing any more photographs from the crime scene. The county wanted a judge to serve a restraining order on the Florida tabloid. The county, said county commissioner Jana Mendez, had reason to believe that the paper had more photographs it had not yet published.

Globe editor Frost said the *Globe* would oppose the temporary restraining order. He said the county's efforts to interfere with the publication might be a violation of the First Amendment.

Sales of the *Globe* were brisk—at least in the places that had copies of it, since Safeway had snatched its copies off the shelves, and the Southland Corporation, operator of the 7-Eleven convenience stores, had never displayed it in any of its 270 Colorado stores. The *People* magazine issue, which did not have crime scene photographs but did have a number of color shots of JonBenét performing in costume, rapidly sold out in Boulder.

Media leaks continued to cause police chief Koby and district attorney Hunter to grind their teeth. Hunter put out a memo to his entire staff reminding everyone that his office had a policy against discussing pending criminal cases. It was the first time Hunter had ever done this, he said.

Police chief Koby, meanwhile, was asked about a *Newsweek* report—unsourced, of course—that fluid found on JonBenét's body had been identified as semen. Further, said the magazine, Boulder police had narrowed the field of suspects down to "as few as seven or eight."

Koby still refused to confirm or deny anything that had been reported.

"It continues to amaze me," he told the *Daily Camera*, "how many 'experts' we have in this thing and how many verifications of information people can come up with out of thin air. With the media, I continue to be impressed by the use of 'sources.' "

Like a crowd following a ball in a tennis match, the focus of the news media now switched back to the Ramsey side of the net, where it was learned, on the same Monday, that the Ramseys had hired a famous former FBI agent, John Douglas, to help investigate JonBenét's murder.

Douglas, who had retired from the FBI a few years earlier, had helped start the Behavioral Sciences Section's psychological profiling unit. He gained fame when it was learned that novelist Thomas Harris had partly based his portrait of an FBI psychological profiler in two best-selling novels, *Red Dragon* and *The Silence of the Lambs*, on Douglas. That made Douglas, at least in the minds of the media, a real person—if his alter-ego was in the movies, he had to be somebody.

During his time at the FBI's Behavioral Sciences program at Quantico, Virginia, Douglas had been part of a team that interviewed nearly three dozen serial and mass murderers confined in various prisons around the United States. The result was a technical study of such killers titled *Sexual Homicide, Patterns and Motives*, in which the family backgrounds of serial sexual murderers were studied and quantified. In a series of interviews with the killers themselves, Douglas and the others worked out a somewhat flexible system for sorting serial crimes into categories, the better to evaluate the sort of person who might have committed the crime.

Generally, the crimes committed by serial offenders tended to fall into two broad categories that could be judged chiefly by the crime scene, by the way in which the body of the victim was left behind by the killer. Douglas and the others, former FBI agent and fellow profiler Robert Ressler, and a psychiatric nurse, Ann Burgess, had concluded that every killer left psychological clues to his identity behind every time he left a victim. The two broad categories of killers, the team concluded, were those crimes committed impulsively and without preparation, and which showed evidence of disorganization or even panic after the commission of the murder; and second, those crimes showing evidence of preplanning, premeditation, stalking, and organized behavior after the murder to cover one's tracks and to conceal the evidence.

Within these two broad categories were two other categories: those killers who wished to conceal their victims for as long as possible and those who wished for the public to learn about them. A serial killer who buries his victims tends to be of the first sort, while a killer like the infamous Zodiac murderer of California, still unidentified, would be an example of a killer wanting the public's attention.

During the 1980s while the study was underway, Douglas found himself consulted more and more frequently by local police departments in baffling serial murder cases. The local departments wanted Douglas to devise a psychological profile of their unknown killer as a means of helping to narrow the field of possible suspects. Sometimes it seemed that the local police had a childlike faith that there was some sort of magic to the profile; most departments were disappointed when the actual document had a marked lack of specificity. Douglas kept trying to tell people that the profile wasn't much good for finding the suspect but was helpful in eliminating people who *didn't* fit the profile; still, local police expected some sort of Rosetta stone that would give them the key to their deadly mysteries.

Douglas's technique was relatively simple. He would obtain crime scene photographs, or even better, videotape, and then, by gazing at the photographs, would try to envision what the killer might have been thinking while committing the crime and afterward. Here, Douglas's experience in interviewing various serial murderers over the years helped put him in the mood and gave power to his extrapolations. He had an idea of how the serial predator thought. Sometimes the course of Douglas's imagination netted real possibilities; at other times, it seemed to the locals, that the result was already obvious: the idea that the killer of a number of women probably hated women seemed pretty clear to everyone from the start, thanks.

Where Douglas excelled, however, was in the

second part of the Behavioral Sciences Section's
mission: the psychological assessment of
known suspects. Since these assessments were
based on known information about a speciifc individual, they were usually far more detailed
and far more accurate as to a specific person's
potential culpability for the crime in question.
Douglas could review this known information
about a specific person and make a fairly accurate assessment as to why or if a particular
person might have committed a specific crime;
moreover, he could provide local investigators
with the sorts of questions and cues that might
elicit a confession. With his experience, once a
suspect was in the net, Douglas could discern
his or her hot buttons and use those to generate
the information the police needed to know.

After leaving the FBI in the early 1990s, Douglas had helped prepare a best-selling book on
his experiences, *Mindhunter*; and had hired
himself out, as had Ressler previously, to legal
experts who wanted the benefit of his profiling
experience in cases involving pathological violence.

Douglas's hiring as the Ramsey Team's profiler seeped out on the Monday when Chief Koby
was bemoaning the rise of ignorant experts
among the media; such was Douglas's cachet as
the model for the intrepid psychological mind-
maven as portrayed in *The Silence of the Lambs*
that the effect was to give the Ramsey side of the
court instant, if temporary, credibility. The im-

port was: if he's hired the man who was the model for *The Silence of the Lambs*, John Ramsey had to be deadly serious in his pledge on CNN to find his little daughter's killer.

"John Douglas is doing some work for us," Korten told the *Post.* "What he is doing is not something I am going to share with you."

What Douglas was doing, however, was fairly obvious: he was meeting with the Ramseys and trying to familiarize himself with their personalities and the contents of the notes left behind by the killer. This was, after all, Douglas's speciality: the psychological assessment. And in taking the job, Douglas was to tell the Ramseys to keep one thing in mind.

"You may not like what I have to tell you," he said.

THE PHOTO CAPER

By the middle of the week, Sheriff Epp had cracked the case of the purloined photos. A Boulder private investigator, Brett Allen Sawyer, and Lawrence Shawn Smith, an employee of Photo Craft Laboratories, the private photo-processing firm hired by the coroner's office, admitted to being the culprits.

Sawyer, a former Boulder County deputy sheriff, Epp said, had been paid $5,500 by the *Globe* for assistance in developing information about the murder and finding photographs. Epp said Sawyer had paid Smith $200 for copies of the photographs, which Smith then provided to the tabloid.

At a press conference, Epp, district attorney Alex Hunter, and Dr. John Meyer, the county coroner, answered questions about the photo fiasco. The news conference was televised live as "breaking news" on CNN.

"I can say," Sheriff Epp said, "that these two people were acquainted with each other before this incident occurred."

After providing details on the charges that had been brought against the two men, Sawyer continued.

"In my twenty-four years with the Boulder County Sheriff's Department I've never seen a case where physical evidence of a crime was co-opted as it was in this case. We needed to apply the appropriate resources to it so that the public trust in the criminal justice system could be restored. This kind of thing brings into question the integrity of the criminal justice system, and because of that we took it seriously.

"In the course of our investigation, we conducted a number of polygraph tests," Epp said. The tests eventually led to a Photo Craft employee, Smith, Epp said. The sheriff said Smith had been arrested, booked, and released pending arraignment on charges of theft, tampering with physical evidence, obstructing government operations, and false reporting. Sawyer had been charged with obstructing government operations and had likewise been booked and released.

Epp turned the news conference over to Alex Hunter, the district attorney. Hunter appeared to be anxious to set the press straight.

"This is my first opportunity as district attorney to speak to the media," Hunter said, "with respect to the *Globe* matter and the Ramsey matter. As matter of jurisdiction, should a case be developed [in the Ramsey murder], it would be handled by my office."

Hunter paused and looked stern as he gazed over the assembled reporters.

"I want you to hear from me," he continued, "that I support Chief Koby in the position he has taken with the media, namely, to hold this case, this investigation, close to his vest. I know that has been frustrating to you in the media. I understand what your responsibility is, but I need to point out, that should the day come when this case is on my desk, I will be following much the same pattern that you have experienced with the chief, and I want to spend a minute to tell you why.

"The rules are very clear in terms of what prosecutors can say to the media," Hunter said. "This is not something that we have developed. It is the result of rules set down by the American Bar Association, rules adopted by the Colorado State Supreme Court."

Now Hunter injected the specter of O.J. Simpson.

"We have seen some big cases in this country," he said. "We've followed them with varying degrees of interest, depending on where we're coming from. I've followed them with great care. I've been the prosecutor here for more than a quarter of a century, and these cases have intrigued me, frustrated me, and concerned me. They have concerned me because some of the recent big cases in the media coverage, have, I think moved away from what the founding fathers and the Supreme Court of this state and the federal Supreme Court have told us, [as to] how criminal cases should be conducted. I think that the people of Boulder, Colorado, and the people around our land, have lost some real confidence in their criminal justice system, as a result of how we all, as a society, how we all, as police and prosecutors, and how we all—and now I throw the media into that—have handled these big cases. And I think we have left the public feeling sort of sad, that we have gotten away from the focal point of doing justice.

"The challenge for Chief Koby, for Sheriff Epp, for me, for my lawyers, for those of us in Boulder County, is, I think to try to do it the right way. To not prejudice the investigation, to not prejudice the case in any manner. That is an enormous challenge but one that is real important, not only for the people of this community, and the people of this state, but for the people of the United States. So, should there be a case, and I pray that there will be a case, I will try to conduct myself according to those rules I've spoken to you about."

The removal of the photos and their publication in the *Globe*, Hunter said, undermined the integrity of the justice system, and thereby eroded public confidence in it.

Even more important, Hunter suggested, the frantic media race to get information was interfering with the public's confidence in the justice system.

"There is really only one ball in the air for me and that's little JonBenét," Hunter said. "That's my focus. I'm not going to be diverted from that course."

After delivering his warning and his lecture, Hunter prepared to take questions.

One of the first was whether the publication of the photos in the *Globe* would hurt the investigation. But Hunter refused to be drawn in to any discussion of the evidence.

"I'm not going to address that at this time," he said.

Asked how his department was led to those who had been arrested, Sheriff Epp said that interviews with the coroner's office staff, supplemented by the polygraph tests, determined that none of the coroner's employees were involved in the leak. Interviews and polygraph tests administered to the Photo Craft staff showed the leak had likely come from there.

The reporters digested this, then tried again to induce Hunter to talk about the murder case.

"Can you give us a progress report on the investigation?" one reporter asked.

Hunter deflected the question. "I have confidence in Chief Koby," he said. "The case is moving forward. I want to preserve the integrity of this investigation. We're taking steps appropriate to this investigation, and that's all I can tell you."

Was Hunter surprised by all the attention that the murder case had generated?

"I don't think so," Hunter said. "As the days have gone by I sort have been catching up, in trying to understand the enormity of the interest. It's understandable, but let's not prejudice the hope that we all have that we can get justice."

Would Hunter agree with criticisms that the Boulder police investigation so far might be an example of "touchy-feely" police work?

"I've seen those criticisms every time there is a big case," Hunter said. "I don't buy it. But I know these people [the Boulder Police] extremely well over a long period of time, and you don't." The allegation that Boulder police were handling the Ramseys too politely was bosh, Hunter indicated.

The rumors and false information published and broadcast in the case were making things difficult, Hunter said. "There's even been a rumor broadcast on one radio talk show that I live next door to the Ramseys," Hunter said. "It's not true, but anything's fair game to that branch of the media."

When asked whether information had been printed or broadcast that he knew was untrue, Hunter said, "There are many leaks that have extremely false information. I really encourage the media to wait until we feel it's the appropriate time. There is a tremendous amount of information out there that's not accurate and it's very unfortunate."

After the news conference, reporters rushed to dig up more information about Sawyer, Smith, and Photo Craft. It appeared from arrest reports that the *Globe* had hired Sawyer to get the photos but told him, or so he claimed, that it had no intention of publishing the pictures, that it only wanted to submit them to Dr. Wecht for his analysis.

One of the first to be reached was Photo Craft president Roy M. McCutchen.

"I am in a state of shock," McCutchen told the *Daily Camera*. "In the twenty-one years I have been the senior operating officer of Photo Craft, nothing like this has ever happened. Our systems and relationships have evolved over years and have been built on the idea that people are basically honorable."

McCutchen said Smith, the photoprocessor, had been fired.

Meanwhile, a Denver television station, KCNC, made contact with Sawyer, who told his side of the story.

Sawyer, thirty-eight, told the station he'd been hired by the *Globe* for $5,500 to obtain any information he could on the murder investigation, including copies of the ransom notes, crime scene photographs, and inside dope from the detectives. Sawyer said it took him only four hours to find out where the crime scene photos were being processed.

Sawyer went to Smith and paid him $200 for copies of the photographs. He told the station that the *Globe* had told him that the photos would only go to Wecht and would not be published.

Sawyer was contrite.

"I don't feel that what I did was right," he told the television station. "I screwed up. I'm accountable for what I did. I made a huge error in judgment."

He would, Sawyer said, give the money he got from the *Globe* to charity. He apologized to the Ramseys.

"I can only ask their forgiveness. I don't expect it. They have my deepest apologies."

Sawyer said that when he learned that the *Globe* would publish the pictures, he called a lawyer, who in turn called the Boulder County Sheriff's Department to tell them what had happened.

But it turned out that Smith, the photoprocessor, had his own twist on the story.

In an interview a few days later in the *Daily Camera*, Smith contended that Sawyer told him he was working for the Ramsey Team of private investigators.

"He said he was working for the Ramseys' independent investigative team," Smith, thirty-six, said. "At that point I didn't see anything wrong. I'd known Brett for a period of years, and

I thought I was helping him out. I never thought they'd be published in the *Globe*."

Thus, there seemed to be a double duplicity at work: if Smith was right, Sawyer had lied to him; and if Sawyer was right, the *Globe* had lied to *him*. All of which seems to indicate why journalists and private detectives might rank so low on the public's most trusted list.

In the flush of recriminations of the photos and the incessant leaks, the *Daily Camera* tried to slam the brakes on what was increasingly looking like a runaway train.

In an editorial titled, "The Rush to Judgment", the *Camera* excoriated the speculative coverage increasingly dominating the story and asked readers to put themselves in the Ramseys' place.

"The brutal murder of a daughter on Christmas night," the *Camera* held, "would be hell on Earth for any family, but in this case it was only the beginning. Recall what happened next as if it happened to you:

"News organizations descend on you from around the world.

"Your personal tragedy becomes the subject of discussion around every water cooler in the country, on every talk show, in every reputable or disreputable media outlet. Photographs of your murdered daughter appear in a tabloid.

"You are subjected to crude amateur psychoanalysis around the clock, by people who have no real idea who you are, and no inkling of your family relationships.

"You know that people are driving by your house, slowly, to satisfy their curiosity about the scene of the crime.

"You realize that some of those people find your behavior 'suspicious.' Whatever the police may think, in the court of opinion you are a suspect."

The Ramseys, the paper concluded, were living a nightmare. The least others could do for them, it said, was back off—just as you'd want others to do for you.

BEAUTY AND THE BEASTS

The tabloid explosion, coupled with the *People* and *Newsweek* articles on the case, renewed attention on the child beauty pageant question.

In a cover piece titled "The Strange World of JonBenét," *Newsweek* took a critical look at the world of child beauty pageants, referring to it as a "subculture . . . that many Americans barely knew existed . . ."

JonBenét had star quality, *Newsweek* said; the flood of professional stills and video proved that. "But," *Newsweek* added, "the effect is distancing rather than illuminating: in all the miles of film that were lavished on JonBenét it is hard to find one frame that captures her soul."

Apart from the question of whether the *Newsweek* writer actually viewed every frame of "all the miles of film" of JonBenét, or how he would recognize JonBenét's soul if he saw it, the point the magazine was trying to make was that JonBenét had, through her participation in the child beauty pageants, been transformed into an object.

"She was rewarded precisely for appearing to be something other than she was, a six-year-old little girl," the magazine said.

An assumption was then introduced through the use of negative linkage: that somehow the transformation of JonBenét into an object was connected to her murder:

"There is no reason to think that her murder had anything to do with her career as a child beauty pageant winner, but now and forever the two images are joined in the public mind . . ." the magazine reported.

This was a backdoor approach to the question of Patsy's involvement in the pageants—as if, somehow, by turning her daughter into what some saw as a sex object, Patsy was partly responsible for what had happened.

The connection seemed to be irresistible, particularly because the linkage between the pageants and the murder provided the media with the opportunity to run and rerun the pageant photographs.

And beneath this approach lay yet another question: was JonBenét's involvement in the pageants a matter of her own choice or was this more the outcome of Patsy's own ambitions? It was as if, by demonstrating somehow that Patsy may have propelled her own child unwillingly into the limelight, she had only herself to blame.

This, of course, is a clear case of blaming the victim or victims.

Nevertheless, attention was focused on the issue of JonBenét's performance and Patsy's role. Was there evidence that Patsy had browbeaten the child or forced her to attend pageants when she didn't want to?

Reporters tracked down a number of people who had been present with their own children in pageants that JonBenét had participated in.

"Everyone who knew JonBenét," *Newsweek* reported, "agrees on what a sweet, normal, well-adjusted child she appeared to be."

In its own piece on the murder, *People* quoted Randy Simons, a professional photographer who had taken many of the images of JonBenét that had been broadcast and published around the world.

"Patsy was your normal mom who absolutely loved her kid," Simons told the magazine.

Diane Hayes, the mother of another pageant contestant, told *People* that Patsy was "not like some of the mothers who are so competitive. Patsy really wanted JonBenét to have fun with it, and she did."

Time magazine, in its piece, found a pageant organizer from Texas who recalled the Ramseys.

"She was such a natural," LaDonna Griego told the magazine. "But she was untouched by it. When JonBenét won, she was just as giddy as the first time, and she was just as happy to be an alternate."

This was pretty much the tone of the main-stream media: that JonBenét had been a natural child, if perhaps a bit too practiced in holding a pose, but still a little girl with a normal relationship with her mother and the rest of the world.

The tabloids, however, weren't going to let this go quite so easily. The *National Enquirer*—without naming any sources—claimed that the authorities had discovered scar tissue that indicated JonBenét had been previously sexually assaulted, and then went on to quote experts in sexual assault cases theorizing that since JonBenét had been trained to "entertain adults," it would have been easy to convince her to participate in sex. There was, of course, no reliable evidence of any of this cited by the *Enquirer*, and the use of the blind quote made it entirely dubious.

The *Globe* also tried to suggest a darker side. In its follow-up issue, the one after the crime scene photos, the *Globe* put a picture of a skimpily clad JonBenét, in her white, feathered showgirl outfit, on its cover, alongside a tabloid-style question-mark headline reading, "Little Beauty Abused Months Before Murder?"

The cover photo was adorned with an arrow and circle, pinpointing what appeared to be a mark on the inside of JonBenét's arm, just above the elbow. "New Photo Evidence" the

Globe reported and trotted Wecht out once more.

"This child didn't hurt herself playing," the tabloid quoted Wecht as saying. "This [the mark] is consistent with someone forcefully holding JonBenét and applying pressure to her arm. You can see that the injury is reddish-purple with a blue tint. It's a fresh wound, and if you look at the curvy linear [sic] aspect of the mark in the middle, you will see what looks like a fingernail digging into it."

The tabloid identified the photographer who took the picture as Mark Fix, and then quoted Fix saying that it appeared to him, when he took the picture in May of 1996, that JonBenét seemed tired or distressed on the day he took the picture.

The *Globe's* foray with the photograph brought an immediate response from one of the Ramsey Team's lawyers, William R. Gray, who apparently had learned of the *Globe's* plans in advance. Patrick Korten posted Gray's letter to the *Globe* on the Rowan & Blewitt website.

"It has come to my attention," Gray wrote to the *Globe's* lawyer, Michael Kahane, "that Globe Communications Corp. may intend to publish one or more stories and photographs of JonBenét Ramsey in beauty pageants with the utterly unsubstantiated conclusion that the photographs provide proof that JonBenét Ramsey was the victim of child abuse.

"Your publication is already aware that a review of medical records of JonBenét Ramsey completely refute this suggestion, that pediatric consultations show no history of child abuse, and nothing in your possession provides any basis whatsoever for a conclusion that Jon-Benét Ramsey was the victim of child abuse at any time prior to December 26, 1996. Spokespersons for the district attorney's office in Boulder, Colorado have publicly stated they are unaware of any evidence whatsoever of a history of child abuse, which conclusion was reached following comprehensive review of medical records and photographs of this child.

"Publication of such clearly erroneous statements in the face of overwhelming proof to the contrary is clearly libelous and in reckless disregard of the truth, for which punitive damages are appropriate.

"Please heed the overwhelming information demonstrating conclusively the falseness of the assertions you appear poised to make, and spare the remaining family members the utterly underserved turmoil, pain, and humiliation which such baseless accusations will produce."

The *Daily Camera's* editorial plea for mercy for the Ramseys seemed to have little effect—at least not on Chuck Green, the *Denver Post* columnist.

On January 17, the Friday following the resolution of the *Globe* photo fiasco, columnist Green broke the story that the FBI's Douglas was actually the Ramsey's second choice as a profiler.

What happened, Green reported, was that the Ramsey's private eye, H. Ellis Armistead, had first approached another former FBI profiler named Gregg McCrary to do the job. But Mc-Crary had turned it down, Green said.

"I thought it over," McCrary told Green, "and I was uncomfortable with it."

Why?

McCrary told Green that he believed the killer would turn out to be someone close to the family. He worried, McCrary said, that somehow he might end up being used to obstruct the prosecution of the killer, "and I didn't want to do that."

McCrary told him, Green said, that a Department of Justice study had concluded there was a twelve-to-one probability the perpetrator would be someone close to the victim—a family member, a friend of the family, or a neighbor. Moreover, McCrary told Green, the younger the child, the greater that probability is.

Green wrote that McCrary went on to provide some of his own psychological assessments of the case:

The fact that the crime occurred inside the family home, McCrary said, indicated that the killer was someone who was "comfortable" in the environment. So did the fact that the note was written there and that a sexual assault had taken place there.

Nor, said McCrary, did he believe that any kidnapping had ever been contemplated by the killer. "Ransom was not a motive in this case. This was not a for-profit crime. That was staging to cover up the murder and to mislead police. And it worked, for several hours."

Yes, said Green, it did.

But this wasn't Green's last word on the Ramseys or the effectiveness of the Boulder Police Department.

Despite Alex Hunter's imploring and Tom Koby's stoic determination to say nothing, the leaks continued to spring the following week.

One of the first to seep out that week was the revelation in the *Denver Post* that the $118,000 ransom demand matched John Ramsey's year-end bonus—a fact that, while known to the police from the beginning, had been kept back for investigative purposes.

Denver Post writer Mike McPhee reported that the bonus had been paid to John by Access Graphics. McPhee didn't belabor the point, but it was obvious that the writer of the ransom note had to be intimately familiar with John Ramsey's compensation package.

McPhee went on to relate some other news: that Ramsey family spokesman Korten had said that John Andrew Ramsey, John's twenty-year-old son with his first wife, had been in the Atlanta area with his mother on December 23, 24, and 25.

"Absolutely," Korten said, "he was with his mother on those days. His mother took him to the Atlanta airport on Thursday, December 26 to fly to Michigan, where he was going to meet his family. When he got to some intermediate point, either his family or friends reached him and told him to divert to Colorado. He arrived in Colorado on Thursday, December 26."

McPhee reported that Korten did not know where John Andrew was at that point in time. McPhee did a little digging and discovered that John Andrew had studied economics at the University of Colorado for three semesters starting in the fall of 1995. McPhee also found out that John Andrew had not preregistered for classes at the university for the coming term, and that he had moved out of his fraternity house "over the Christmas break." The university had sealed John Andrew's student records at the request of the Ramsey family, McPhee reported.

And there was one other development, McPhee said: there was "tension" between district attorney Alex Hunter and Ramsey spokesman Patrick Korten over the issue of whether JonBenét had been subjected to child abuse.

In fact, after reading Ramsey lawyer Gray's letter to the *Globe* about the issue, Hunter repudiated Gray's statements.

"We have issued no such statement [that authorities were unaware of any child abuse]," Hunter said, "and I have authorized no such statement from my office."

So that meant there had been evidence of child abuse? Not necessarily, only that no one from Hunter's office had ever said there was no such evidence. Thus, Korten and Gray seemed to have been caught going a bit too far.

Korten tried to recover.

"The fundamental facts remain true that there was never any abuse," he said. Korten said he hoped to resolve the discrepancy over who had said what about abuse within the next few days.

To McPhee, Korten also seemed to show signs of irritation that the investigation was taking so long. He told McPhee, "I see a point coming shortly where the family will be excluded as suspects."

How shortly?

Korten paused and stared at the ceiling, McPhee reported. Then Korten spoke. He didn't mean to say shortly, Korten said; he only meant to say that he anticipated that the police would exclude the family. But, said Korten, no one on the Ramsey side knew what the police had, because no one was sharing any information with them.

Finally, McPhee reported one last bit of news: the police had asked the Ramseys to sit down for a formal, videotaped interview and to take polygraph tests. "The family," McPhee reported, "has not granted either request."

*   *   *

That development was columnist Chuck Green's cue. In a column in the *Post* on the same day as McPhee's story, Green blasted both the police and the Ramseys for the delay in scheduling a formal interview session.

"When's the Interview?" Green's column was titled.

"Despite police chief Tom Koby's insistence that his officers have conducted their investigation 'by the book,' " Green wrote, the Boulder police had failed to follow appropriate investigative procedure from the beginning. He knew this, Green wrote, because he'd asked his pal, former FBI agent McCrary, what should have been done.

And McCrary had told him that the Boulder police should have separated all members of the Ramsey family immediately on hearing of the kidnapping and begun interviewing them simultaneously. The police, Green said McCrary told him, should have considered two possibilities from the start—that maybe there had been a kidnapping, and maybe there hadn't.

All of which caused Green to propound the question to Koby:

"Just what was the name of that book you followed, chief?"

ABUSE BY LEAK

As the direct result of Ramsey lawyer Gray's letter to the *Globe* and Hunter's repudiation of its central assertion, the suggestion that JonBenét had experienced child abuse soon rolled over into the mainstream media—in the *Daily Camera*, no less.

"'Authorities are investigating the possibility of past child abuse in the murder of JonBenét Ramsey,' sources said Thursday," the paper reported on Friday, January 24.

The paper contacted Ramsey family friends and confirmed that investigators had asked them questions about possible abuse. Those quoted by the *Camera* derided the suggestion of abuse within the family.

"They asked me," said Shirley Brady, the former Ramsey nanny, "if the first divorce ended because of child abuse or if I had heard anything about child abuse ever mentioned. And they asked me how the children acted when they were around their daddy."

After reprising the salient facts of the dispute between Gray and Hunter, *Daily Camera* writer Alli Krupski turned to "a source" who said that investigators had looked for evidence of abuse from the beginning.

"We want to make sure we're covering all our bases. We have not ruled anything out," Krupski was told.

Korten said the Boulder authorities had JonBenét's medical records, and the records showed no abuse. But a city spokesman, Kelvin McNeill, refused to comment one way or another on whether the records had been turned over.

All this unfolded the day after the *Rocky Mountain News's* Charlie Brennan had broken still more details about the murder. From this point forward, Brennan began to scoop his opponents at the other newspapers fairly consistently.

First, Brennan's new information included "SBTC"—the first time that the Subic Bay Training Center abbreviation, as used in the ransom note, had been published. Brennan was able to confirm that John had been stationed at Subic Bay from 1968 to 1969.

Brennan also reported that there were four misspellings in the note, another piece of news that had been kept back. Investigators, Brennan said, believed that the misspellings were deliberate, as part of an effort to conceal the writer's identity. Brennan noted that the word "attaché," as in case, was spelled with an accent over the final "E." That made investigators believe the note writer was smarter than he was trying to portray.

Further, Brennan reported, the investigators believed that the cord tied to JonBenét's wrists may have been tied there after the murder to make it look as if a real kidnapping had been attempted.

In the week that followed, Brennan obtained tips on equally sensitive information; it is therefore fair to raise the question of why this was, and what it might mean.

Taking all of the leaks together, those to Brennan and to the other newspapers as well, one consistent pattern about their nature seems to have been present almost from the very beginning: that is, the leaks all tended to involve information that brought the investigation ever closer to the Ramsey home and the Ramseys themselves.

There was, for example, little leakage in terms of others who might have had keys to the house or a familiarity with it; or sexual predators known to be in the Boulder area; or about others familiar with Access Graphics and John Ramsey's compensation package.

The bits that were leaked, taken together, painted a portrait of a killer who was at ease in the house, who knew its floor plan, who knew the patterns of movement of the occupants, and

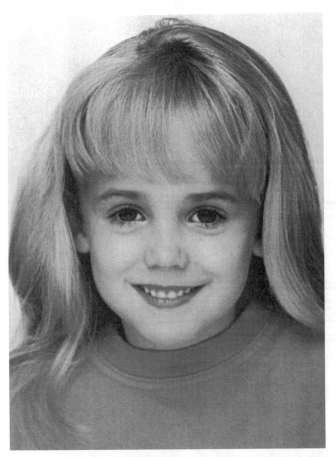

Six-year-old JonBenét Ramsey was found dead in the basement of her family's home in Boulder, Colorado, after her mother found an abduction note and reported the girl missing to Boulder police. (*AP/Wide World Photos*)

JonBenét Ramsey was
named Little Miss
Colorado in 1995.
(*Gamma-Liaison*)

Little Miss Colorado in full pageant costume. *(left: Gamma-Liaison; below: Sygma)*

Ramsey family photos: *(Right and below)* Burke, and sister JonBenét. *(AP/Wide World)*

(Right) The Ramsey family. Top left to right, stepsister Melinda, father John, and stepbrother John; front row left to right, JonBenét, mother Patricia, and brother Burke. *(AP/Wide World)*

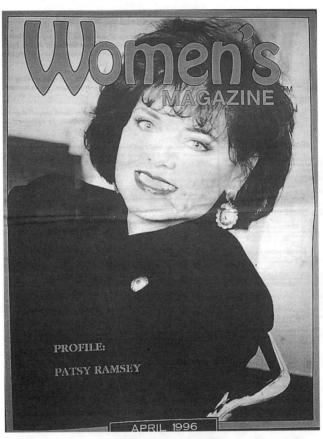

Patricia Ramsey graces the cover of *Women's Magazine*.
(*Gamma-Liaison*)

The body of JonBenét Ramsey is led out of the Peachtree Presbyterian Church in Atlanta Tuesday, December 31, 1996. (*AP/Wide World Photos*)

Colorado Episcopal Bishop Jerry Winterrowd greets John Ramsey and his wife Patricia after church services at St. John's Episcopal Church in Boulder, Colorado. (*The Denver Post*)

Lab agent Kathy Dressel works on DNA evidence at the forensic lab at the Colorado Bureau of Investigation in Lakewood, Colorado. (*AP Photo*)

A magazine rack at the checkout counter at King Soopers grocery store is absent of *The Globe* in Boulder, Colorado. King Soopers and other major grocery stores in Colorado refused to sell *The Globe* after they obtained and printed photos that were taken at the murder scene where JonBenét Ramsey was found strangled. (*AP/Wide World Photos*)

A handmade cross rests against Christmas decorations outside of the home of JonBenét Ramsey. (*AP/Wide World Photos*)

who knew things about John Ramsey that no stranger would ordinarily know. The squabble over potential child abuse was still another leak—or at least inference—that pointed to the Ramsey family.

The bald fact about leaks to reporters from confidential criminal investigations—or for that matter, almost anything confidential—is that almost always such leaks are committed by a person with a motive for telling. The leaker wants to see something happen from his or her work in telling the media. The task in evaluating such leaks is to discern what the leaker hopes to accomplish; unfortunately, in the world of journalism as practiced today there is far too little assessment of what such leakers may hope to accomplish.

It is rare that such leaks are made out of a sense of civic duty—especially when the police chief and the district attorney are threatening discipline on anyone who violates the orders for silence, while laboring mightily to avoid prejudicing their investigation. And despite what newspaper reporters might like to believe, people don't leak to them because of their winning personalities or even their sheer persistence in badgering sources.

One way of looking at the motive for leaks is to assess the results. In the case of JonBenét's murder, the overall effect was to tie the case closer and closer to the Ramsey family; the net effect of this inevitably put more political pressure on Koby and Hunter to move the case toward arresting one of the Ramseys. To this point, however, Koby and Hunter had resisted any such pressure; the leaks were therefore continuing, leading to such criticism that the police were "touchy-feely" toward the Ramseys. Fairly blatant assertions were shouted at press conferences that the Boulder cops were handling the case with kid gloves because of Ramsey's wealth and influence.

It is likewise clear that the leaks had to be coming from someone familiar with the details of the crime scene and the overall case. Chief Koby had already removed one detective from the case, Sergeant Mason, and "sources" had told the newspapers that the removal was because Mason was suspected of leaking to the press. Mason, in fact, had hired an attorney to contest his dismissal.

Mason, of course, was familiar with the details of the case as they were being reported by Brennan, McPhee, and others. If Mason or someone similarly unhappy with the chief were doing the leaking, why would the information have dribbled out over the weeks, as it had, instead of all at once? One possibility is that the leaker, whoever it was, was dealing his or her facts off one by one, attempting to get the maximum publicity for each leak and thereby slowly building political pressure on Koby. The fact that Koby—a 1991 hire as police chief and not a native of·Boulder—continued to receive the overt political support of Mayor Leslie Durgin and City Manager Tim Honey seems to indicate the possibility that a political struggle was underway between elements of the Boulder Police Department and the city's hierarchy, with the Ramsey case forming the fulcrum of the dispute. In other words, every new leak that tied the murder closer to the Ramsey family put even more pressure on the Boulder city officials.

In the aftermath of all the leaks, the Ramseys' Korten told reporters that the family wanted to get back to normal as soon as possible. The Ramsey family, it was reported in both the *Post* and the *Daily Camera*, expected John Ramsey to return to work at Access Graphics in Boulder. The word was the Ramseys were going "stir crazy" while waiting for the police to complete their investigation.

"Ramseys Edgy as Probe Plods," headlined the *Post*. Ramsey spokesman Korten said the family was trying to avoid the news media by staying with various friends in the Boulder area. It couldn't have been very much fun, moving from safehouse to safehouse like spies on the lam.

"It's still tough," Korten told the *Post*. "So much time away from their friends and their community is making them a little stir crazy." Korten said he was trying to preserve the other Ramsey children's privacy as best he could.

John, Korten reported, hoped to return to his

job at Access Graphics. On such a prospect, reporters from some television outlets staked out Access Graphics in the hope of getting some video. One reportedly got into the rear stairwell of the building but was discovered and ejected.

Laurie Wagner, spokesperson for Access Graphics, said the company would try to return to normal when John Ramsey returned. The company would not make John available for interviews, she said.

But the word that John wanted to go back to work didn't sit well with at least one disturbed individual. On Friday, January 24, the same day that the abuse allegations surfaced in the *Daily Camera*, a man called Access Graphics and told the telephone receptionist, "You [expletive expletive], if you let that [expletive] back on Monday, you're all dead."

No Autopsy

O n the Sunday following the bomb threat, the *Post*'s Green was back in the Ramseys' faces.

In a column titled, "Ramsey Team—Quit Whining," Green said the Ramseys' reluctance to submit to a police interview was "curious at best, inexcusable at worst."

Given the lack of a formal interview, Green continued, the Ramseys' lawyers and consultants ought to quit complaining that the investigation was taking too long.

The fact that the Ramseys had hired a team of lawyers, private investigators, handwriting experts, and the former FBI profiler John Douglas, all to "second-guess" everything the Boulder police had done and were doing, Green said, was the main reason why the police were taking so long.

"Now," said Green, "if they don't take their

time, they can be accused of making a rush to judgment.

"Sound familiar?"

Meanwhile the autopsy of JonBenét's body had continued to drag on for several weeks as medical officials sought to perform additional tests, which no one, not even "sources," seemed willing to enumerate.

While normally autopsy reports are public record in Colorado—they aren't in every state—Boulder County officials said they intended to go to court to have the final report sealed when it was completed.

That posed a problem for profilers like Douglas, who needed the autopsy to help his reconstruction of the crime.

Douglas had spent "four or five hours" with the Ramseys over the weekend; additionally he had met with Boulder police. Exactly what was accomplished with this meeting was unclear, although it appeared that Douglas was given little if any information by the police. It sounded as though Douglas had given the Boulder police the benefit of his own generic insights into such sex murders, but that was about it.

On that Monday, January 27, a new flap blew up when the *Rocky Mountain News*'s Brennan learned that the DNA tests on the fluid found on or near JonBenét's body hadn't even begun.

In his story the following day, Brennan quoted a "source close to the Ramsey family" as saying the fluid sample was so small the Colorado Bureau of Investigation laboratory would likely have to consume the entire sample to do the tests. Because, Brennan reported, Colorado law required such tests to be performed in the presence of counsel for a defendant, and since there was no defendant as yet, the tests could not begin.

Not everyone, however, agreed with this analysis. In fact, the director of the CBI lab said that such an assertion was nonsense. The director, Carl Whiteside, said the state did have the right to make the tests simply because there was no defendant.

"We think the law is clear," Whiteside told the *Post* the day after Brennan's story, "that if someone has been charged with a crime and the tests consume the sample, they [the defense] has a right to have their experts here during the testing process. In the absense of a defendant . . . we would conduct that test and consume that sample regardless."

The *Post* also reported that the Ramsey side wanted to be allowed to monitor any DNA tests, attributing this to "sources," but then said that neither the Boulder County District Attorney's office or Korten would confirm such a demand. It was, it appeared, another leak.

The subject of leaks was taken up by Chuck Green on the same day.

In "Leaks the Only News We Get," Green recognized that leakers come fully equipped with motives.

"Nobody talks to a reporter without a motive," Green said.

And while some leakers are motivated by the purest of intentions, Green said, "most sources have ulterior motives."

One of the main ulterior motives, Green said, was the old reliable: money. But just because a leaker gets paid doesn't always mean the leaker is lying, Green said. In fact, he said, he'd met plenty of leakers who lied for free.

Meanwhile, John Douglas had been doing some leaking of his own. He'd been a guest on *Dateline NBC* the previous Monday and told the world that he didn't believe that John Ramsey had committed the murder.

"I just don't believe in my heart that he did this," Douglas said during the program. He'd spent four or five hours with both of the Ramseys, Douglas said, and if either of them had killed their daughter, "they have to be the biggest liars in the world."

His assessment of the murder, Douglas said, was that the killer may have been an Access Graphics employee or former employee angry at John Ramsey, who struck at JonBenét to get revenge.

The killer, Douglas theorized, had followed the press and "what's going on in Boulder. There's been a lot of publicity that the child is a precious posession of the Ramseys, and what better way to get back at the Ramseys is—is to kill that child."

But that didn't track: the problem was there had been no publicity about JonBenét in Colorado prior to her death.

Douglas also put his foot in it when he implied that he had reviewed the autopsy data on JonBenét, or at least, that was the implication drawn from his statements. It would later come back to haunt him.

His four or five hours of conversation with the Ramseys, was, however, entirely consistent with the FBI's normal profiling process: sitting down with suspects, conducting an interview, and then determining whether the suspects had the psychological makeup to have committed a specific crime.

He had been retained by the Ramseys, Douglas acknowledged, when some Boulder police investigators formed the theory that John had been the murderer.

The way this fact slipped out—after all, it was the first time anyone even semi-officially connected with the case had confirmed that police were suspicious of John Ramsey—was fairly amazing.

After so many days of hinting around the subject, it's a bit surprising that no reporters confronted Chief Koby or even the infamous "sources" to find out whether this was true: that police had at one point told the Ramseys they were suspicious of John.

One possible conjecture related to this may be used to account for the severe leakage marking the investigation so far. It is possible to theorize that one or more Boulder officers had become suspicious of John's involvement in the murder fairly early—perhaps as early as the day the body was discovered; further, it's possible to theorize that an investigator, embarrassed by the gaffe that permitted John to discover the body and remove it, in reaction had focused on John too soon—at least for Chief Koby's comfort.

In turn, as Koby insisted that all of the forensic evidence testing be completed before any action, a frustrated police officer or officers may have begun leaking crime scene details in order to embarrass Koby and push the chief off the dime.

But the import of Douglas's casual assertion that the police suspected John slipped by the news media, which fastened instead on Douglas's claim that he was familiar with the autopsy results.

How could that be, if the autopsy hadn't yet been completed?

The day after Douglas's appearance on *Dateline NBC*, reporters peppered the coroner, Dr. John Meyer, with questions. Was it true Douglas had seen the autopsy report?

The *News*'s Brennan reported that coroner's

officials denied having discussed their autopsy findings with Douglas; furthermore, Brennan said, the Boulder County District Attorney's office likewise denied discussing the case with Douglas.

So did the police.

"Third-party investigators have not been provided any information that has not been provided to members of the media or members of the public by the police department," said Boulder spokesman Kelvin McNeill.

So far, of course, the only official information that had been released was that there had been a reported kidnapping attempt, that JonBenét had been murdered by asphyxiation, that no arrests had been made, and the investigation was continuing.

The coroner, Dr. Meyer, confirmed that the autopsy still had not been completed.

HOLLYWOOD GUY

Two days after Douglas's appearance on *Dateline NBC*, some of the FBI's old dirty linen began to unravel in Boulder. It turned out that some of Douglas's old comrades at the Behavioral Sciences Section didn't like Douglas very much.

In a story headlined "Profiler a Hollywood Guy," the *Post*'s McPhee reported that not only wasn't Douglas the Ramsey Team's first choice, he wasn't even second.

McPhee said the Ramsey Team had first approached something called "The Academy," which he identified as an organization of eighteen former FBI and Secret Service agents "who hire out around the world as investigators and profilers."

Everyone at "The Academy," McPhee reported, had turned down the Ramseys' offer of employment. McPhee dug up Douglas's old running mate, Robert Ressler, for comments on Douglas.

"Douglas is more into entertainment," Ressler told McPhee, and for the likes of the FBI, there could be no more cutting a comment.

McPhee also noted that Douglas was coming out with a new book, *Journey into Darkness*, and had been scheduled to sign copies of the same at a Boulder bookstore on February 20. McPhee's clear implication was that one reason Douglas had taken the Ramsey job was to hype his book sales.

Ramsey spokesman Korten played down the significance of the new Douglas book. Douglas, Korten said, "is not riding the notoriety of this case."

On the same day, *Post* columnist Green jumped in. In "Profiler Slipped Up," Green suggested that Douglas had put his mindhunter where his mouth was.

Green resurrected McCrary, the former FBI agent who had initially declined the Ramseys' offer, and said McCrary had found flaws in Douglas's work for the Ramsey family.

Douglas's gut belief that the Ramseys weren't guilty wasn't enough, McCrary opined.

"I've talked to guilty offenders in the penitentiary," McCrary told Green, "and some of them are so manipulative and persuasive they almost have you believing they didn't do it."

McCrary told Green he didn't buy Douglas's theory that JonBenét's killer was trying to get back at John Ramsey. Citing the reports of sexual assault, McCrary contended that the motive was sexaul psychopathy, not revenge.

If it had been revenge, McCrary continued, the killer would have displayed the body, not hidden it in the wine cellar. If the killer wanted revenge, his objective would have been to "shock and offend" John Ramsey.

Moreover, he noted, a revenge killer wouldn't have stopped to write a ransom note.

That may have been McCrary's most telling point: if the motive had been revenge, why wouldn't the note have referred to revenge, rather than a kidnapping that had never taken place?

But given the fact that no one had yet officially confirmed that a sexual assault had taken place, and that McCrary had not seen the ransom note—as Douglas had—it was also possible that McCrary was wrong.

The next night, Douglas was a guest on *Larry King Live*. King introduced Douglas while a file videotape showed coroner's office staffers wheeling JonBenét's body from the Ramsey house on the night after Christmas. Among the other guests were Brennan, CNN's Brian Cabell, both speaking from Denver, and Los Angeles lawyer Leslie Abramsom, along with former Los Angeles County Superior Court Judge Jack Tenner. The appearance gave King a chance to plug Douglas's new book, *Journey into Dark-*

ness, a sort of tour of the personalities of a number of serial psychopaths.

King asked Douglas how he had been brought into the JonBenét Ramsey case.

"The only thing I can say," Douglas said, "is that the attorneys requested me, brought me in. They brought me in to do an objective analysis of the case, and I will say that when I was brought in, because I heard some of my former colleagues, and people get the impression, well, here's a hired gun going in . . . Well, if they say that, they don't know this John Douglas, because my whole career in the FBI, I would say things that even the FBI didn't like."

He wasn't the sort of person who would tailor his conclusions for anyone, Douglas indicated.

King asked Douglas if he believed that John Ramsey was involved in the murder of his daughter.

"If he were involved," King asked, "you would report that to the authorities?"

"Definitely," Douglas said. "And I told them, you can buy my time, you're not going to buy my opinion, or am I going to risk my reputation?"

King asked Douglas what his role was in the investigation and whether he was hired to provide a psychological profile.

As he often did in the past when such a question was asked, Douglas winced a bit. It was difficult for people to understand that a psychological profile was only part of a behavioral analysis of a crime, and perhaps not even the most important part. But *The Silence of the Lambs* had made it difficult for people to understand.

"Really," Douglas said, "to profile who killed the little girl, I would need more information. But what I can do is, is I can certainly begin to eliminate some people, and look on the surface the type of people who perpetrate these types of crimes, and that was my role."

Douglas had apparently told King that he couldn't speak specifically about the Ramsey case, because the Ramsey lawyers had told him he might wind up being a witness in the case, possibly in a Colorado grand jury inquiry into the murder.

Well, said King, did Douglas believe the Boulder police were close to an arrest?

Douglas said he couldn't say. He hadn't been in close contact with the police for some days. But Douglas said he believed the case was eminently solvable.

"They have a lot of evidence," he said, "and they're dealing with a very small community, and I would put my money on the police to come up with a solution."

Why was it taking so long? King asked.

Douglas said he thought there might be several reasons for the delay. One, he said, might have had to do with contamination of the crime scene.

"It's a dilemma," he said. "If you have a contamination of the scene by family members, police, ministers, touching the body, walking over the potential evidence, that will cause definite forensic problems in the future."

King asked if Douglas had definitely eliminated John and Patsy as suspects.

"Yes, I have," Douglas said. "I will say that, I have excluded the parents."

King: "So even though they've hired you, that's not the reason you've eliminated them?

Douglas: "No way, if you believe in what you do, that's the way it is, no matter who was criticizing you."

Douglas then noted that child murders involving molestation very frequently involved killers who knew the victim very well. Often, he said, such killings take place as a result of stress. A killer may have a number of "stressors," as Douglas called them, working at once, and one may prove to be the precipating cause of the murder. A person, he said, might lose his job, be in financial difficulty, be facing a divorce, or have some intense personal problem that triggers sudden violence. Holidays can themselves be a stressor, Douglas said.

At this point, the Los Angeles lawyer Leslie Abramsom, who defended Erik Menendez, jumped in. She wanted to know just how Douglas had eliminated John and Patsy, in the absense of DNA test results.

"I'm dying of curiosity to know on what basis you eliminated the parents, when there's been no DNA testing, and we know they were in the house, so they had the opportunity. What was the basis of the elimination?"

But Douglas declined to be more specific, except to say that he'd interviewed hundreds of violent offenders, which implied that on the basis of his four or five hour interview with the Ramseys, he'd concluded that they just did not have the capacity to commit the crime. That was an analysis that could be reached through the interviewing techniques, along with an assessment of the ransom note.

Abramsom said she thought the whole situation at the Ramsey house was strange, what with the ransom note and the body being found at the same location. Douglas agreed.

"It tells me," he said, "that things were staged. The other thing is motive. What was the motive?"

After more discussion about the O.J. Simpson civil trial jury, which was still out at the time of the broadcast, and the problems in the FBI's crime lab, King turned to CNN's Cabell and the *Rocky Mountain News*'s Brennan.

"John Douglas," Cabell said, "is subject Number One in Boulder. He's been talking and talk is indeed about him."

What were people saying? King asked Cabell.

"A number of people have said he's been hired," Cabell said, in reference to Douglas's statements clearing the Ramseys. "And there are questions of acccess." Cabell said people wanted to know whether Douglas had been given inside information by anyone to warrant his opinion about the Ramseys.

Now Brennan had his shot at Douglas.

"I've been trying to reach him for a little while," Brennan said. "The big question out here is, who briefed him [on the autopsy report]?"

"I was briefed by the attorneys," Douglas replied.

The Ramsey lawyers? Brennan persisted.

"For Ramsey, yes."

"You never said you'd read the autopsy report, did you, John?" King asked.

"No," Douglas said. "I never said it. A lot of people think you have to be at the scene, read the material, [but] as long as someone can tell you, can describe something, you can do an analysis."

But that only sparked Abramsom, who asked Douglas how the Ramsey lawyers could have briefed him on the autopsy when the report hadn't been completed.

"That's the question," Brennan said.

All Douglas could do was reiterate that it hadn't been necessary to see the report, only to get a description of the crime scene, which he'd certainly gotten from the Ramseys themselves, if no one else.

WRESTLING WITH RESSLER

In the midst of all of this, Boulder County officials moved to induce the courts to seal the focus of all this debate, the autopsy report.

The county attorney filed a motion seeking the sealing because, it contended, the report contained details that might compromise the murder investigation.

"During the course of investigation of this death," the county's motion read, "evidence and witness statements may well be obtained that will be either contradicted or corroborated by the confidential information contained in the autopsy report. Disclosure of the confidential information that will be contained in the autopsy report jeopardizes the ability of investigators to gather evidence and pursue leads."

The county lawyers said Dr. Meyer's office anticipated completing the report by February 12.

They wanted a hearing on the motion to seal on that date.

The newspapers said they would object to the sealing, and the battle lines were drawn once again between the authorities and the news media.

What did the county attorney's office mean? What was there about the autopsy report, the disclosure of which would endanger the "ability to gather evidence and pursue leads?"

A hint is offered in the language employed by the county attorney's office. Witness statements "will be either contradicted or confirmed" by the autopsy results. That was a sign that any evidence of previous sexual and physical abuse, if it ever happened, would be played against witness statements denying such abuse. If such abuse could be scientifically documented, that had the tendency to put such denials in the light of possible deceit. Deceit could be a part of probable cause to seek arrest. That was why the county lawyers wanted the autopsy to remain sealed—likely pending the formal, videotaped interview with the Ramseys, the interview that had not yet been scheduled.

Meanwhile, Ressler wasn't done with his old friend Douglas. Ironically, his dig about "Hollywood John" rang a little hollow when Ressler came to Boulder to do his own behavioral assessment of the crime for a television program.

The *Post*'s legal affairs writer, Howard Pank-ratz, interviewed Ressler.

Ressler's first point was that JonBenét's killer almost certainly was someone she knew. He was convinced, Ressler said, that the killer was someone in JonBenét's "immediate circle."

That circle, Ressler opined, would include the Ramsey family, neighbors, and friends of the family. Also, workers in the Ramsey household and adolescent boys living in the neighborhood. Ressler added another category as well: John Andrew Ramsey's fraternity brothers.

The circle seemed to be getting larger and larger the more Ressler thought about it.

"I draw the line," Ressler told Pankratz, "at making any pointed directions at any one person. The only thing I will say is I feel that the person knows the child . . . and I think the entire kidnap note, the garotte, the rope, the whole thing I think was a staging to cover up the true motivation and to cover up the identity of the person who committed the crime."

Ressler told Pankratz that he'd never seen a case like the Ramsey murder. "It is highly, highly unusual," he said.

Ressler said he was nonplussed by the idea that the killer felt comfortable enough in the house to hang around and write the bogus ransom note.

The staging of the note was the best evidence the police had, Ressler said. Simply analyzing the "psycholinguistic" tendencies revealed in the note ought to narrow the focus on suspects down considerably.

Ressler said he didn't believe that the killer meant to kill JonBenét. Here again he differed with Douglas, who believed the murder was committed to get even with John Ramsey.

Ressler said he thought the murder was an accident. In this, Ressler sounded a bit like Dr. Wecht. An "accident" in which a victim is subjected to duct tape and a garotte, as well as a sexual assault—if indeed those reports were accurate—seemed more like a sex game gone wrong. On the other hand, there was no evidence that the duct tape and the garotte had come after the smashing of JonBenét's skull—which would make it part of the staging, not the crime itself.

What did all this psychological mumbo-jumbo really amount to?

The simple fact was, none of the experts—not Douglas, not McCrary, not Ressler—had any real way of making any sort of useful assessment. None of them had seen the crime scene as it was discovered by John Ramsey and Fleet White. None of them had read the autopsy report. Only one, Douglas, had had the opportunity to interview two of the principal witnesses, John and Patsy. As Douglas had admitted on *Larry King Live*, he simply didn't have enough information to draft a psychological profile. Neither, for that matter, did anyone else, including the police, who, after all had still not formally interviewed John and Patsy. As for McCrary and Ressler, they had even less information.

So what was this all about? Why were these experts pontificating about staging, and comfort, and people close to the family, or revenge, or sexual psychopathy? It was, in a way, not really all that much different than when the news media sends its reporters into the street to ask the ordinary person what they think about something. Most of the time the ordinary person doesn't have a clue, but such is the lure of putting one's two cents into the public domain no one is able to resist sounding off about things.

That seemed to be true about the "profiling experts," as well. The only real difference between them and the man-or-woman-in-the-street was that they were billed as experts by the media. They used words like staging and comfort and all the rest, as if they were saying something new, but it wasn't really anything more than a statement of the obvious. Thus did the experts and the media use one another as America tuned into another day of the Information Age.

INFORMATION CHAOS

That the murder of a six-year-old girl in a small town in Colorado could generate such intense interest across a nation and the world stands as only the most obvious sign that the world we live in is vastly different than that of even a generation ago.

For one thing, news of such a murder likely would not have ever crossed the Colorado state line fifty years ago. Even if it had, it would likely have earned only one or two small newspaper stories, to be clucked over, and then forgotten, as people turned to their own very real concerns in their own very real lives.

What's changed everything is television.

Through the magic of this increasingly technologically sophisticated medium of communication, we today experience a connectedness undreamt of by our grandparents. Even as late as the 1950s, to paraphrase a famous politician, all television was local. The race to the moon changed all that.

Through the miracles of miniaturization ushered in by the race to the moon, the television camera metamorphosed from a gargantuan box to a device that can be held, if need be, by one hand. Like the broom of the sorcerer's apprentice, the camera multiplied uncontrollably. Barriers of time and distance collapsed, cultures began to be amalgamated, we woke up to see two-dimensional neighbors we never before had. And still don't, despite the illusion that what happens in a small town in Colorado is our business.

For most Americans, the dawn of the Information Age came with the first dose of what has come to be called reality TV, the assassination of a president, and the first "real-time" murder ever seen on television, the murder of the assassin, Lee Harvey Oswald. Within a decade Americans had the spectacle of a war in their very own living rooms, courtesy of the Pentagon and the networks. And as the seventies turned into the eighties, still the shrinkage continued, from Watergate to Three-Mile Island to KAL 007 to Iran-Contra to Operation Desert Storm. We sit in front of boxes, in "real-time," feeling superficially connected to one another with the aid of the curiously named "remote."

And with the flood of images, information, and instant analysis, comes confusion. We long for something, someone, to sort through the welter, to reassure us that things can't possibly be so out of control as our boxes make them seem. And the media tries hard to oblige, employing increasing numbers of people, often rude and poorly trained, to ferret out new bits of information that will explain all those bits that have come before. The result, however, is simply more of the same insensible and often senseless tintinabulation, sounds and fury signifying nothing of real importance.

What's been lost in the Information Age is, paradoxically, time. While information flows faster, one would think one had more time, but the opposite is true. As our sensers overload with streams of facts and pictures, we lose our capacity to let events unfold, our capacity to balance the conflicts, to sit back and reflect on the deeper meaning of events.

The crowding together of so many images, of so much contradiction, of so much Babel, has naturally encouraged an incipient desire on the part of many people for simple explanations: even sinister simplicity, the kind that leads people to find conspiracies in everything. Thus some people believe in black UN helicopters, or space aliens, or the Illuminati; the list of possible simple explanations—which, being unverifiable, embrace everything—is as limitless as the Information Age itself.

We want the answers, and we want them now, so we can go back to being puzzled by something new. And when the system doesn't give us our answers, our surrogates, the news media, will howl on our behalf.

So it was with JonBenét Ramsey, a little girl found dead in a place called Boulder, Colorado. The public demanded answers, if for no other reason than to go on to the next sensation; and when the powers-that-be couldn't immediately provide the answers, people began to see the dark and simple, and to cry out: what was taking so long?

It was, in fact, the following week after the *Larry King Live* show, that the imperious demand for answers came to the CNN television show, *Burden of Proof.* Veteran O.J. commentators Roger Cossack and Greta Van Susteren expressed amazement that nothing had yet happened in Boulder.

Cossack: "Greta, aren't you surprised, with all the clues they seem to have in this case that they haven't gotten very far?"

Van Susteren: "Roger, I think it's stunning, the fact that they haven't arrested someone. You have a letter, which has handwriting analysis, which has possible fingerprints, you can lift fingerprints from paper, you have DNA, you have fibers, you have knots, you have ropes, you have location of the body. The only thing you don't have is someone with a sign that says 'I did it.' I think it's stunning that this hasn't been solved so far. I don't know what's taking so long. There must be some problem with the investigation we haven't heard about."

Well, there wasn't much problem with the investigation that no one had heard about. The problem was with the Ramseys, and the awful fact that trace evidence from John had likely been transferred to JonBenét's body when he picked her up. That meant contamination of the evidence, and it could have been avoided had the police acted appropriately the afternoon of December 26. The possibilities were ominous: that the Colorado Bureau of Investigation would find evidence that they might improperly use to link John to the murder; or worse, that the evidence was so worthless that the killer, whoever he or she was, could not be convicted.

The Ramseys' position in all this was clear, even understandable, if one takes the time to appreciate it, as if there were no Information Age. A horrible, stomach-wrenching tragedy had befallen them. Even an outsider—as most people were—could be physically sickened by the notion of a little girl, slowly being choked to death in her own house on Christmas night, particularly if one had the capacity to imagine what must have been going through her mind as the horror unfolded, which can hardly bear contemplation. Take that feeling and multiply it a thousand, even a million, times, and one might approximate how the Ramseys must have felt.

And then, to find oneself targeted as the possible perpetrator—to be thrown up to the wild currents and vicissitudes of the news media's

voracious demands—would be even more ap-
palling. Under such circumstances, the idea
that the Ramseys would hire lawyers and investigators and spin doctors hardly seems unusual; indeed, from the perspective of the
Information Age, it seems the only safe thing to
do, if you can afford it.

Yet it has to be said: the Ramseys' posture toward the authorities, however well-thought-out,
was one of the prime reasons it was "taking so
long."

From the much-maligned Chief of Police Tom
Koby's point of view, there was no hurry, other
than the artificial deadlines imposed by the
clamoring crowds, for "rushing to judgment." If
the Ramseys turned out to be somehow responsible for JonBenét's death, they weren't going
anywhere. And it was hardly likely that more
such murders would take place while the investigation proceeded. Koby's job was simple: get
the evidence and get it right.

If that meant asking the Colorado Bureau of
Investigation to test, test, and test again; if it
meant waiting for weeks for those test results to
be completed so that a formal interview with the
Ramseys could be scheduled, Koby was prepared to wait. As he pointed out over and over
again, his obligation was to JonBenét Ramsey,
and no one else.

THE LAW OF INJECTION

One other aspect of the Information Age soon came into play in the JonBenet Ramsey murder case, and it might be called the Law of Injection.

It's hardly surprising that, as an event looms ever larger in the public mind, some individuals are driven to inject themselves into the mix. Serial murder cases, for example, are notorious for attracting all manner of seemingly ordinary people who want to participate in the uproar. The bigger the story, the more such people clamor to climb aboard—and often in the strangest of ways.

The *Daily Camera*'s Elliot Zaret touched on this phenomenon in a piece the paper published on Monday, February 3. In "Ramsey Mystery Attracts 'Sleuths,' " Zaret discussed how the paper's own Internet website had become a "gathering place" for people to speculate about

JonBenét's murder, and to proffer possible solutions.

Zaret found a professor of media psychology in Los Angeles, Stuart Fischoff. The murder case, Fischoff contended, "fills a kind of gossip gap. There's a strong entertainment value, even if it passes as compassion."

The *Daily Camera* had also been contacted by telephone by a variety of people from all over the country, Zaret reported. One man from the Midwest told the paper that he had an idea of who the killer was. It seemed that a man in his hometown had recently skipped out after a suspicious fire that had taken place after the businessman had failed to raise $118,000 to complete a business deal.

"That's what tipped me off," the Midwestern "sleuth" told the *Camera*: the coincidence of the same amount of money. The Midwesterner told the paper that it seemed clear the absconding businessman had gone to Boulder to kidnap JonBenét and hold her father up for the badly needed $118,000.

Not least among the injectors were the psychics. Zaret reported that a Florida woman claimed to be in contact with JonBenét. The woman told the paper that JonBenét said she'd written the ransom notes herself! Worse, the whole thing was making her sick, the psychic said.

That was one facet of the injectors; sooner or later the exterior events that had grabbed their attention were turned inward toward the injector's own problems. It was as if the murder of JonBenét had happened for the injector personally.

"You're tapping into a segment of the population that doesn't have a lot in their life," Fischoff observed. Injecting oneself into the case, he added, "gives them meaning. Their personal identity is somehow tied in the case."

The newspaper wasn't the only one getting crank calls. A great many people decided to go directly to the police with their contributions. By early February, Boulder spokesman Kelvin McNeill said that the police department had received an estimated 1,300 telephone calls about the murder, and 600 letters.

"To date," McNeill said, "only five percent of the calls and letters have warranted some form of follow-up." What McNeill didn't say was that even taking the time to evaluate the surge from the injectors took time.

Tuesday, February 4, brought forth still another apparent leak from the investigation. Both the *News*'s Brennan and the *Post*'s Pankratz had stories reporting that investigators believed that JonBenét's murderer had "wiped" her body with a cloth that left fibers behind.

Both reporters contacted Ressler to ask what he made of this development.

Ressler said the wiping of the body indicated that the killer felt "psychological remorse or concern." That, in turn, underscored the idea that the killer was someone who knew Jon-Benét, Ressler indicated.

A stranger, Ressler said, would be less likely to do something like that. A serial predator almost certainly wouldn't do it. Cleaning the body after the crime, he said, would be more consistent with someone who had concern for the child.

Brennan added that "sources" wouldn't say whether the cloth used for the wiping had been recovered, but noted that if it had been, it might prove to be important evidence. If, for example, the cloth came from the house—or perhaps consisted of clothing belonging to a person living in the house—that would again bring the focus back to those who had been in the house on the night of the murder.

The following day, February 5, a Boulder judge sealed the search warrants and supporting affidavits for another fifteen days. The newspapers were not happy—especially when the judge, Diane MacDonald, wouldn't even allow the lawyers for the newspapers to present their argument against the sealing.

Tom Kelley, a lawyer representing both the *Post* and the *Daily Camera*, said he was shocked that the judge wouldn't even listen to him.

"That's not the way the system is supposed to work," Kelly told the *Post*.

The sealing only made things worse, not better, Kelley contended. In the absence of reliable information because of the sealing, the news media had resorted to leaks. Leaks, Kelley said, can come from people with ulterior motives.

"The Supreme Court of the United States has recognized that the essential function of the press in reporting crime is to cover what happens in the courts," Kelley said. "This is how the system is supposed to work, and is far preferable to reporting leaks."

Too bad, said the lawyer for the Boulder County District Attorney's office, Laurence DeMuth. The sealing continued to be necessary because disclosing the information might "compromise the validity of witness statements to law enforcement."

There it was again: the suggestion that the authorities had information from the autopsy that they did not want the Ramseys, or anyone else, to know they had, the better to interview them.

But there still seemed to be little movement toward getting the Ramseys together with the police—and, indeed, there was no way for the police to force the issue. There is no law that requires anyone in the United States to talk to the police if they don't want to.

Korten, the Ramsey spokesman, said that the Ramseys would sit down with the police, once a "suitable agreement" could be worked out between the Ramsey lawyers and the police.

A suitable agreement? What did that mean?

It fell to the *Post*'s Chuck Green to shed some light on that.

In a column titled, "Discrepancies About the $118,000," Green at first appeared to soften his confrontational stance toward the Ramseys, only to whack them again by suggesting that John Ramsey had been untruthful with John Douglas.

"'John and Patsy Ramsey have desperately wanted to talk to police, but they have been held captive by their attorneys,' a source close to the family has said," Green reported.

According to Green's source, the Ramsey lawyers had thwarted the long-awaited interview because they feared that the Boulder police would twist the Ramseys' words against them. If Green's source was accurate, that sounded like the Ramsey lawyers were convinced that the Boulder police were determined to pin the crime on the Ramseys.

Green reported a few other details about the case that hadn't yet surfaced.

The last time anyone other than the killer saw JonBenét alive, Green said his sources told him, was around nine P.M., when JonBenét was put to bed. She had been carried half asleep into the house by her parents after the family had visited friends Christmas night. Conceivably, the footprints in the snow that had been so meticulously measured by the police on the day the murder was discovered could have been those of the Ramseys themselves, returning to the house after their Christmas visit.

But Green was troubled by something Douglas had said John Ramsey had told him during their four or five hour interview. Douglas told the *Dateline NBC* program that John had told him that Access Graphics had paid $118,000 into John's 401(k) retirement account at the end of the year.

But a pension expert told him, Green said, that "there is no way this sum could be deposited into a 401(k) for Mr. Ramsey." Such a large amount far exceeded the amount allowed by Internal Revenue Service regulations.

"Was Ramsey innocently mistaken," Green wrote, "or did he lie to Douglas?"

Because Douglas had cited the $118,000 "401(k)" disbursement to Ramsey as evidence that the killer was likely to be someone connected with Access Graphics—perhaps a fired former employee—the fact that such a statement by Ramsey was possibly inaccurate could question John's credibility, and by extension, Douglas's assertion that he believed John wasn't the killer.

But with this argument, Green seems to have leaped over another possibility: that Douglas, not always known for the precision of his words, had simply misstated what had been told to him by John Ramsey; that Ramsey might have told Douglas that the money had been paid into his retirement account, and Douglas simply assumed this was a 401(k).

This only illustrated the problem all over again: no direct contact with the source, and interpretations of interpretations driving the machine.

MORE MUD

The approaching end of the week brought another outpouring of dubious product from the supermarket tabloids, which, if anything, were becoming even more daring and invasive.

The *National Enquirer*, for example, seemed to flatly tell its readership that Patsy was going to divorce John. One had to look close for the qualifier: "Friends fear . . ."

The *Enquirer* produced a former Ramsey household employee the paper identified as Linda Hoffman-Pugh, and said that Hoffman-Pugh claimed that JonBenét was a chronic bedwetter. This, the *Enquirer* informed its readers, was evidence that JonBenét had been the victim of child abuse. The tabloid produced experts to back this up.

The paper went on to use more blind quotes that contended that the Ramsey marriage had been failing even before the murder. Since the murder, the tabloid reported, Patsy and John no longer trusted one another, a statement which served to imply that each of the Ramseys thought the other had done it.

The *Star*, meanwhile, implied it had an exclusive: an actual interview with Patsy. They quoted her saying that she felt her life was over. A closer reading of the *Star*'s account, however, showed that the words attributed to Patsy had come from a third person, a minister the paper said was friendly with Patsy. The paper said it had tracked the Ramseys down to a friend's house on the outskirts of Boulder, and produced a photograph of same to illustrate its dogged persistence.

In a series of quotes the paper said were Patsy's own words—but which actually came from the minister, who claimed to be relating what Patsy had told *her*—an image of Patsy emerged of an emotionally exhausted woman weeping inconsolably day after day, while a helpless John stood by, unable to do anything to help his wife feel better, while anxiously wanting to return to work as soon as possible.

And in an interesting aside, the paper reported that police had warned officials of the University of Colorado to be prepared for a future announcement "which could embarrass the university."

What was all this about? With the usual technique of implying something without actually saying anything, the *Star* refocused attention on

John Andrew. The paper said John Andrew had dropped out of sight after the police had taken samples of his hair, blood, and handwriting. The reporting contrived to make the suggestion without actually saying that John Andrew was back in the frame as a suspect.

One result of the tabloids' coverage was to influence the mainstream media's own rumor mill. Soon, talk was circulating that John Andrew had been in Boulder on the day of the murder, after all. The Ramseys, through their spokesman, Korten, angrily denied this.

The *Globe* went even further. In its story, question-mark headlined, "Did Daddy Do It?," the *Globe* said flatly that the Boulder police had targeted John as the killer.

"Amid fears parents are splitting, detectives believe father is key to little beauty's savage murder," the *Globe* said.

The *Globe* went one better than its competitors when it quoted a Ramsey neighbor, a Boulder lawyer. "It would not shock me," the paper said the neighbor told them, "if Mr. Ramsey is the murderer. The fact that he seems to be a successful, respectable businessman means nothing. You can never tell what internal demons a person is battling."

"Clearly," the paper quoted the neighbor, "John and Patsy know of something they are not telling the police."

With friends, neighbors, and ministers like these, it was no wonder Patsy was weeping uncontrollably, if she was. To have all this dredged up and thrown out into the public domain was sickening, even if it were all true. If it wasn't, it was even worse.

But the tabloids knew one thing, and that was those color photographs of JonBenét were good for their bottom line, and to them, that was what really mattered. Even the *Globe*'s offer of a $50,000 reward for information leading to the arrest of JonBenét's murder had a crass commercial quality to it; the paper had offered $200,000 for the arrest of Ennis Cosby's murderer, which only seemed to indicate that at the *Globe*, everything had its price.

As the week wound down, the rumor mill churned on. Gossip married speculation, and produced the bastard offspring of rumor. The talk was that an arrest was imminent.

The rumor about a forthcoming arrest was given more substance by the fact that Boulder City officials admitted they were preparing for just such an eventuality.

A spokeswoman for the Boulder County Commissioners, Janna Peterson, said she'd been contacted by District Attorney Alex Hunter and asked to "begin figuring out what the logistics of handling a major case like this would be."

Peterson told the *Post* that the biggest anticipated problem would be, naturally, handling the news media.

"There are a number of concerns," Peterson

said, "mostly logistics, like parking, cameras in the courtroom, the size of the courtroom, and credentialing." Peterson said the county had been in contact with other places that had had similar high-profile trials, including the Polly Klass murder case in California, and the trial of Susan Smith in North Carolina.

Was an arrest really about to take place? No one knew, for sure; or at least, no one who did know was talking. Reporters plumbed their "sources," but for once, the leaks seemed to have dried up. All anyone could do was point to the fact that the forensic tests were due back the next week from the Colorado Bureau of Investigation. Maybe then, the reporters told one another and their audiences, something would happen.

But over the weekend a new wrinkle was added to the case: Police, the city confirmed, had received a letter from an unknown person about the murder, and wanted very much to find out who the person was.

THE LETTER

The mysterious appearance of the anonymous letter caused the rumor mill to grind to a sudden stop: How did this new development fit into the preexisting speculation? It was an X factor.

According to Boulder City spokeswoman Leslie Aaholm, the letter had arrived at the Boulder Police Department after having been postmarked in Shreveport, Louisiana in late January.

"The letter," Aaholm said, "contained potentially significant information which is of interest to Boulder investigators."

The Boulder police had been in contact with their counterparts in Louisiana for help in tracking down the identity of the letter writer. The reason, Aaholm said, that the city was revealing the letter's existence was the hope that the letter writer would see the news coverage and contact the police directly.

What could this letter possibly have contained? What significant information would someone in Shreveport, Louisiana, know about the murder of a little girl in Colorado?

Even the origin of Shreveport wasn't necessarily a clue, Aaholm said. "It could have been written in Seattle, flown to Shreveport, and mailed there," she told the *Post.*

A Boulder detective, Steve Thomas, asked that the public "respect the investigators' time and resources and call and write only if, in fact, you are the author of the letter."

Here was the Law of Injection at work once more; Thomas knew that the chances were, the police would net a number of contacts from people claiming to be the letter writer, if only to get some attention from the police.

"This is not a request," Thomas said, "for unsolicited or psychic information."

Ramsey spokesman Korten said his clients were as baffled about the Shreveport connection as anyone. He told the *News* that the family knew no one in Shreveport, and that they had no idea what information the letter might contain. Korten said he understood why the police wanted to minimize the response to their request.

"We've had our share of psychics at this end," he told the *Post.*

And besides the psychics, he added, the Ramsey side had its hands full trying to squash rumors that kept erupting. One rumor that had just cropped up, he said, was that the Ramseys planned to exhume JonBenét's body and have it examined by their own pathologist.

"Utterly, utterly, false," Korten told the *Post*. "Not even a tiny bit of truth to it. I honestly would like to know where these things get started."

The following day, new speculation was reported about the mysterious letter. The *Post*'s Marilyn Robinson reported that "a source" told the newspaper that the letter was written by a person who claimed to have had a child in a beauty pageant that had also had JonBenét as a contestant.

That was it.

The single, simple fact that the letter may have had something to relate about the beauty pageant business appeared to tie the murder once more to the pageant world. Out came the photos and the videotape once more, along with speculation about the connection, if any, between the Ramseys and the pageants.

Meanwhile, city spokeswoman Aaholm was shooting down rumors as fast as they flew up. One was the rumor about John Andrew's whereabouts on Christmas Day. Aaholm had said as early as December 30 that the police had determined that John Andrew and Melinda Ramsey had been in Atlanta on the night the murder occurred. And she was sticking to that, she said.

"I have not had anyone suggest," she told the *Post*, "that I was given wrong information or that I should retract what was said earlier—and that that is now in doubt. So we are holding by that original statement."

And from Atlanta, Cindy weighed in on this point as well.

In an interview with the Atlanta *Journal-Constitution*, Cindy said both John Andrew and Melinda had been with her over Christmas. The day after Christmas, even as the events were unfolding at the Ramsey house in Boulder, John Andrew and Melinda were on their way to the Atlanta airport to catch a flight to Michigan, where they planned to join their father. When they arrived in Minneapolis, they learned for the first time of the reported kidnapping. They then made new arrangements to go to Denver instead, where they took a cab to Boulder.

Given their presence in Atlanta on Christmas Day, it was impossible for either of the two older Ramsey children to have been in the Boulder house at the time of the murder.

By Friday night, CNN's Larry King apparently felt the need for a summing up of the situation. In a segment of his show, *Larry King Live*, he interviewed a *Newsweek* reporter, Daniel Glick, along with the *Rocky Mountain News*'s Brennan.

"In a late development, investigators say there

could be an important aspect to this case, a letter postmarked Shreveport," said King. "Daniel, what's that all about?"

"Good question," Glick said. "Police received an anonymous letter that was postmarked January—excuse me, December 27, that's the day after the murder. They won't reveal what the contents are. They've been trying to find out who wrote that letter."

"So they had to use the public," King said.

"Right," said Brennan. "They had to use the public, and as with most other aspects of this case, they're using more of the public or getting more of the public than perhaps they wanted." Brennan said he believed that the police were being "inundated" with calls from the public about the letter, thanks to the instantaneous communications made possible by modern media.

"Daniel," asked King, "What's the guessing game? As to what this could be?"

"Well," Glick said, "the guessing game, at least in my book, is if the police department, the Boulder Police Department, is relying on an anonymous letter coming from Shreveport, Louisiana, to crack this case right now, they're in a lot of trouble. My guess would be, I hope it's not of any terrific significance for them to make an arrest."

Brennan said he agreed with Glick. He noted that the city had received nearly 600 letters, and that the police had said about five percent of the letters and calls contained information that required followup. To him, Brennan said, that meant the police had thirty letters containing some sort of worthwhile information.

"As Dan said," Brennan remarked, "if they're looking at this letter that closely right now, it would seem to put the lie to stories that we're hearing all week long that an arrest is imminent." All those reports, Brennan added, were coming from the media, not from officials.

"Daniel," asked King, "is there any uproar in the community, like 'Find the killer!'"

"There's a drumbeat," Glick said, "a sense that we're closing in on something. Some of the [forensic] tests are coming back. One would hope, that if this is someone close to the family, as we've been told all along, that they would be close to an arrest. As far as an uproar, people want it to be over."

"Charlie," said King, "the tabloids are having a field day, are they not, with the father?"

"Well, they certainly are," said Brennan. "As I have said from the beginning, I've learned that a lot of the tabloids are reporting things that may have some merit, some other things I know they have reported are offbase. It sort of almost seems to be an approach of, throw as much as you can at the wall and see what sticks. It cannot be emphasized enough that the police have never publicly identified anybody as a suspect, or ruled anybody out as a suspect, and sure, the tabloids are hammering on the family, and it'll be interesting to see how their stories are reading should this case have some other kind of conclusion."

"Of course," said King, "today the implication is the father knows who did this and is covering up for who did it. Is that pure speculation to you, Daniel?"

Glick agreed with King that that was one theory being floated about the murder, but he said there were so many theories, it was impossible to put credence in any single one.

"One thing that we do know, we've said this all along and the police have said it, the odds of this child's killer being known to the child are very, very high. And whether that means the father knows too, one would presume yes," Glick said.

"Do you expect some news soon?"

"We've had several rounds now," Glick said. "A couple of weeks ago it was reported on one of the local television shows that Mr. Ramsey had turned himself in. Then last week one TV reporter came on the air and said an arrest was imminent. We keep hearing this but sources close to this are not confirming there's anything imminent. At this point I guess you'd have to say you hope there's something imminent. But these kinds of investigations can go on for months."

"Charlie, can this really go on and on and on?" asked King "It seems, for want of a better term, solvable."

"Well it certainly seems solvable," Brennan agreed.

"I mean, it looks like a *Columbo*," King said.

"Yeah, it does," Brennan said. "I mean one of the better *Columbo* episodes, at that. It's worth noting that the city was making preparations for press conferences and press briefings—how they will be handled in the event of an arrest." He'd checked with city officials, Brennan added, and police sources confirmed that they were making such plans. But, said Brennan, he was told that the plans may not be needed for another two years.

King gave off a grunt that sounded like incredulity, and asked the question that had so perplexed CNN's Cossack and Van Sustren: what's taking so long?

Glick offered an opinion.

"From the very beginning," he said, "two initials have really haunted the Boulder Police Department: O.J."

The police, said Glick, wanted to make sure everything was right before moving ahead.

But there was a curiosity about this discussion. While Boulder spokesman Leslie Aaholm had said the mysterious letter was postmarked late in January, Glick said the letter was postmarked in late December—"the day after the murder," as Glick put it. Who was right?

It didn't sound as if Glick had misspoken,

since he had pointed out the proximity of the letter to the date of the murder.

The timing of the letter was significant. Generally speaking, a communication from a witness tends to lose its relevance the longer after an event that it's received. By late January, there had been so much leaked about the case that it was possible the letter writer had read or heard enough to cobble something together that sounded reasonable. That was one reason why police had wanted to keep so much secret: to distinguish between what a witness might actually know, and what they had come to believe because of all the news coverage.

But if the letter indeed had been postmarked on December 27, not January 27, as Glick was saying, the likelihood of its usefulness would be greatly enhanced. After all, at the early date, very little had leaked out about the murder. This might tend to show that the letter writer indeed had pertinent information.

Beneath was another puzzle. If indeed the city of Boulder wanted the letter writer to come forward to be interviewed, what was the use of saying that the letter had been postmarked a month after it had actually been mailed? Was that any way to get the writer to come forward? Wouldn't the writer conclude that it must be some *other* letter the Boulder people were talking about?

The whole thing was curious, and Aaholm was not immediately available to clarify the situation, as the effort to find out who killed JonBenét Ramsey rolled into its sixth week, with forensic reports due to be returned by the Colorado Bureau of Investigation.

And if the reports didn't provide clear evidence of who had murdered JonBenét, what then? It was, as Charlie Brennan told Larry King, possible that it might be a very long time indeed, before the whole truth was known.

PAGEANT ABUSE

As noted, the sudden appearance of the mysterious letter renewed interest in the child beauty pageants which so marked the short path of JonBenét's life. If the anonymous writer was, in fact, the mother of one of JonBenét's child competitors, what, if anything, did that mean?

Two possible scenarios were bruited in the news media: one, that the letter had come from someone who was jealous of JonBenét's pageant triumphs; and second, an idea marshalled by the *Daily Camera*'s Alli Krupski, was the idea that the letter writer's child might have talked to JonBenét before her death, and that JonBenét had said something significant in that conversation. This latter possibility skirted the question of whether someone had abused JonBenét, and that JonBenét may have said something about it in the weeks prior to her death.

"There's a possibility it's someone from the pageant circuit," Krupski quoted an unidentified source. "It apparently said something about JonBenét sharing information with this person's child, or some other details that may be useful in solving the case. But until you find the author, it really makes you suspicious as to how believable it is."

The *Post*, meanwhile, floated the idea that the letter was somehow connected to the Miss U.S.A. Pageant, which had just been completed in, of all places, Shreveport, Louisiana. The pageant ended February 5, after nearly two weeks of activities in and around Shreveport—activities attended by dozens of small girls with their parents, who'd come to see what the big show was all about, along with thousands of adults focused on the pageant itself.

Like Krupski, the *Post*'s Pankratz also reported that a source had told his newspaper that the letter had come from someone who claimed to be the parent of a child who had once competed in a pageant entered by JonBenét.

As for the critical question of when the letter had been mailed—December or January—Boulder spokeswoman Leslie Aaholm said she believed the January date was correct. And despite Brennan's prediction in the *News*, the public's response to the police plea for assistance was hardly overwhelming, she said.

"We've had a whopping two or three calls," she said on the Monday after the Friday plea for assistance.

Was the world of child beauty pageants somehow connected to JonBenét's murder? After all, JonBenét had competed in pageants all around the country, including Michigan, Georgia, Tennessee, and Florida, as well as Colorado. That could encompass a large universe of potential letter writers. And, as some pageant directors had noted in *People*, *Newsweek*, and other publications, there were some parents who resented JonBenét's talent, and who had pulled their children rather than let them lose to JonBenét.

Still, the notion that JonBenét's murderer might be a deranged parent seeking revenge for a loss in a beauty pageant seemed to fly in the face of all the experts' prognostications—that the murderer was someone who knew JonBenét and her family intimately.

Nevertheless, the underside of the world of child pageants still bears looking at, as much for what it says about the psychological environment of JonBenét's murder as anything else.

In the initial aftermath of the murder, when *People*, *Newsweek*, *Time*, and every other mainstream media outlet jumped all over the beauty pageant aspect of the case, a subtle tripwire was yanked: that the killing of JonBenét was somehow the result of her success as a child beauty.

One couldn't point to any logical progression of facts that led to this conclusion. Rather, the juxtaposition of the photos of JonBenét and the reality of her murder raised the question, which was never answered overtly, but only subtextually: act like a sexy little girl and you run the risk of becoming the victim of a sex murderer.

At this point the feminists deserted JonBenét Ramsey: while widely deploring the fact that she had been so elaborately made up and costumed, and had been trained to sing and dance, those who criticized JonBenét's nascent career as exploitation failed to defend her right to do so without being murdered. In other words, regardless of whether one thought it was appropriate for JonBenét to be dressed in such a fashion, the fact remained that it certainly should not have been a death penalty offense. JonBenét had the right to dress and act as she chose without being murdered for it, exactly the same argument that enlightened people grant to adult rape and murder victims said to have dressed provocatively.

At least part of this problem of perception was the photographs of JonBenét. In the weeks after the murder, a photographer who took many of the most visually arresting images of JonBenét, Randy Simons, sold his portfolio to a New York agency for $7,500. Those images, along with others taken by another photographer, Mark Fix, were the ones that found their way into magazines such as *People* and *Newsweek*, as well as the supermarket tabloids.

In an interview with the *Post*, Simons said he'd been offered up to $100,000 for the pictures. He wasn't interested in the money, Simons said; he only wanted the pictures to be distributed worldwide "so this guy [the killer] would have no place to hide."

Just how worldwide exposure of his photographs of JonBenét would unmask the killer was unclear.

Simons said that after the news about the murder broke, he contacted the Ramseys to see what they wanted him to do with the pictures. A Ramsey family friend told him to sit on the pictures for a while to give Patsy Ramsey "time to heal."

"I locked them in a bank vault," Simons told the *Post*, "and figured I'd just sit and wait for the media to find me and hold them off as long as I could. I also wanted to make sure I wasn't trying to hide. I realized it was going to make me look suspicious if the media wanted these so bad and they couldn't find me." Simons said that while he waited, insinuations cropped up that he was trying to conceal the photographs because they showed evidence of child abuse.

That wasn't the case at all, Simons said. As far as he could see, JonBenét was a perfectly normal child, although unusually talented.

A few days later, Simons again spoke to the *Post*, when reporter Bill Briggs examined the whole issue of child beauty pageants.

His photographs of JonBenét were not sexy, Simons insisted.

"We're doing art," he said, "not painting makeup on this girl. Anybody who can look at that and think it's sexy, maybe they should reevaluate themselves."

Still, the issue of child sexual abuse, connected with the pageants, kept coming up, especially in the supermarket tabloids.

As noted, the *Globe* had quoted Dr. Wecht as saying that the crime scene photographs indicated to him that JonBenét's killer had been engaged in a sex game with her when the murder occurred.

And in its January 28 issue, the *National Enquirer* contended that the Boulder Police had searched the Ramsey house with infrared lights and fiber optic cables to see if there were any hidden rooms or storage spaces. The *Enquirer* seemed to imply that police were suspicious that evidence of sexual molestation, such as photographs, might be hidden in the house.

The tabloid went on to report that the searching police located "revealing" pictures of JonBenét in the house, but didn't attribute this information to any named source.

"They show a sequence in which she's posing in a bikini," the tabloid quoted another unnamed source. "And there are shots of her topless as she changed outfits."

Perhaps to their credit, none of the mainstream media mentioned any of these supposed "revealing" photographs, and in the absence of police comments about the case, it was unclear whether this was just more of the mud that the *News*'s Brennan was talking about, or if there was anything to it.

That was also the situation regarding the mysterious letter as the first week of February neared its end: It simply wasn't clear whether the letter was someone's attempt to inject themselves into the case, or if there was any real value to it. And when a Denver area television station reported that the anonymous letter contained an assertion that JonBenét had confided to another child that a family friend had abused her, the police declined to say anything at all.

KOBY

As the Ramsey case entered its seventh week, it was becoming more and more clear that Boulder Chief Tom Koby was the man on the spot.

Koby, after all, was the one who was in charge of the police department, and if the department had botched the case at its inception—and no one was ever charged and convicted—Koby was the one most likely to get the blame.

"Koby," wrote the *Post*'s Pankratz on February 9, "has positioned himself as the lightning rod for the JonBenét murder case, as much for his method of refusing to say a word about the investigation as his refusal to name even a suspect or rule out anyone, including family members."

In a profile of the chief, Pankratz went on to describe Koby as "smart, savvy and self-assured," a "90's-style cop" who was more a manager than the "old-style beer-bellied flatfoot" who had spent three decades walking a beat before moving to the top job.

That certainly seemed to be an accurate thumbnail description of the Boulder chief—more of a systems man than a pistol-packing crime fighter.

In many ways, Koby's experience and philosophy meshed well with an upscale, environmentally aware and technologically sophisticated town like Boulder.

Koby was a part of the new wave of policing in the United States: so-called community policing, in which police get out of their patrol cars and interact with the public on a wide variety of problems, not simply criminal offenses. One of the key tenets of community policing is that police and public alike need to cooperate in responding to "quality of life" problems—little things such as overgrown vacant lots, broken windows, public drunkenness, and panhandling, that, if left unaddressed, can give rise to far larger problems as public apathy sets in.

Koby was 47, and a native Texan. He grew up in Houston, and became a cop in that town in 1969. By the end of the 1970s, Koby had risen to the rank of lieutenant; he had also obtained a degree in business administration from the University of Houston. The education in management was particularly useful to Koby as the Houston department struggled to adapt to changes in the 1970s and 1980s.

By 1985, Koby had become commander of the

Houston police department's burglary and theft investigation division. Outside of traffic control, there's probably no other aspect of policing that lends itself so well to modern management practices as property crimes. Because property crimes generally have an economic motive, organizing information about such crimes lends itself well to pattern analysis: where the crimes most frequently occur, how the stolen artifacts are disposed of, the relationship between stealing and drugs; all can be effectively analyzed to allow a police department to fine-tune its resources for best effect. Koby did this well enough to be named the department's manager of the year in 1985.

The Houston chief at the time was Lee Brown, who later became police commissioner in New York City, and after that, the so-called federal drug "czar," in charge of U.S. efforts to combat the spread of illicit drug use. Brown thought Koby was sure to become the Houston chief one day.

By 1987, Koby had become an assistant chief in Houston. At that point Koby and other up-and-coming officers instituted the community policing philosophy in Houston. Not everyone liked the new concept, particularly older officers, who tended to see community policing as a waste of time and an interference with their real job, which was to catch bad guys.

Still, Koby remained well-regarded by the Houston police department's rank-and-file,

mostly becase of his nonconfrontational, cooperative style.

When Brown left for New York, Koby hoped to
be chosen as the new Houston chief. But some
of the controversy over the community policing
philosophy continued, and eventually Koby
withdrew his candidacy for chief. Koby said he
couldn't work for Houston Mayor Kathy Whitmire, because Whitmire hadn't provided enough
support for the department.

Koby then applied for open chief's jobs in Colorado Springs and Boulder. He was hired by
Boulder City Manager Tim Honey in 1991.

After taking over as chief, Koby restructured
the department's training regimen; he also displayed a certain political acumen by doing away
with the department's Police Explorer program,
because of the national scouting program's refusal to admit gays and lesbians.

One of Koby's actions also demonstrated his
community-oriented approach to policing.
Problems caused by underage drinking are en-
demic in many university towns, and it appears
that Boulder was no exception. Rather than
simply attempting to enforce the drinking laws,
Koby got the cooperation of university officials
to begin an education campaign aimed at re-
ducing underage drinking. The university officials made it possible for Koby to coordinate
with fraternity and sorority leaders at the university so that such college traditions as beer

parties might be reduced or at least better controlled.

In any event, the murder of JonBenét Ramsey certainly represented Koby's biggest test as a police chief; and as the *Post*'s Pankratz noted, Koby was in a tough position: if someone were arrested and convicted, it would be District Attorney Alex Hunter and his deputies who would get all the glory; but if the evidence was too weak and there was an acquittal, "Koby will take the hit."

None of this appeared to bother Koby. However, as noted from the beginning, Koby had insisted that the case would be investigated "by the book," despite the rocks coming his way from the news media.

Koby's relationship with the news media appeared to turn sour as the legions of outside reporters flooded into the town. At one point during his televised news conference early in January, Koby touched on this when he observed that from then on, it was going to be Boulder against the world—meaning all of the outsiders who wanted to come crashing in to demand things and otherwise subject the police department and the town itself to merciless scrutiny.

However, Koby's by-the-book mentality soon brought him disparagement when during his press conference, he, in typical police-speak, referred to JonBenét's murder as an incident.

"We were managing an incident," Koby said,

in response to questions about what the police did and when they did it.

The *Post*'s Green took issue with Koby for that atttempt to maintain the standard police emotional neutrality.

"Officially speaking," Green wrote in the January 12 edition of the *Post*, "the brutal and heartwrenching death of JonBenét Ramsey was not a murder.

"It was an incident."

But Koby's image troubles didn't begin or end with Green. In the January 20 issue of *Time*, the magazine's former managing editor, James R. Gaines—who had just moved to Boulder—chastised Koby for presuming to say that the murder of JonBenét was really only the business of Boulder residents, and no one else.

"Let's get this straight," Gaines wrote. "Chief Koby believes that this crime belongs to Boulder and that the rest of the country is just rubbernecking. Hello? Maybe I am new here, but when I think about JonBenét Ramsey, it is not a matter of prurient curiosity; I'm wondering what to believe in."

The country had a stake in the solution to JonBenét's murder, Gaines went on.

"Evil on this scale is impossible to comprehend," Gaines wrote. "To know who murdered JonBenét Ramsey is to know what world we live in, where we are."

And Gaines added that the news media didn't

come flooding into Boulder because they had "kinky appetites; we go because we are sent."

As the seventh week of the investigation proceeded amidst all the unconfirmed anticipation of an arrest, it developed that the hold-up on the long-awaited police interview with the Ramseys had at least something to do with the location of the interview: the police wanted to conduct the interview at police headquarters, but the Ramseys didn't want to go there.

Ramsey spokesman Pat Korten told *Post* writers Kerri S. Smith and Mary George that the Ramseys were eager to talk, but that negotiations on where to hold the interview had bogged down.

"Are we willing to negotiate the terms of such an arrangement? Of course we are," Korten said, "and we always have been. While we're happy to talk, we're not going to come to police headquarters."

The *News* had a slightly different take on the interview situation. The paper said Korten contended that the Ramseys had offered a formal interview "some weeks ago and it was rejected." Korten said the Ramseys wanted to do the interview somewhere else to avoid a media circus.

This was, to say the least, a peculiar situation. What difference did it make where the interview was conducted? Indeed, a strong case could be made that the best place to conduct the interview would be at the Ramsey house—still unoccupied after the murder.

By conducting separate videotaped interviews with both Ramseys in the house, the police would have the opportunity to question each Ramsey about their movements; even, indeed, to ask them to replicate their movements during the hours in question. Additionally, if the Ramseys were somehow involved in the crime—as John Douglas had suggested the Ramseys believed that the police believed—placing potential suspects in the emotional environment where the crime had been committed was excellent interviewing technique.

So what was this all about? Why did the police insist on conducting the fabled interview at police headquarters? Or *had* they insisted on this? Koby's people refused to comment.

Meanwhile, in another development, the media circus finally became too much for a Ramsey friend.

Jay Elowsky, the owner of Pasta Jay's restaurant that John Ramsey had invested in, was arrested by the Boulder police when he chased three men, one of them a television sound technician, away from his neighborhood with a baseball bat.

It appeared that reporters suspected that Elowsky knew the whereabouts of the Ramseys, and that some believed Elowsky was bringing the Ramseys food from his restaurant and from church volunteers. Some reporters staked out Elowsky to follow him back to the hidden Ramsey lair, which some suspected was Elowsky's own house in north Boulder. The *Post* reported that a car belonging to Donald Paugh, Patsy's father, was parked at the house on the day of the baseball bat imbroglio.

In his statement to the police, Elowsky said he saw people walking around in his backyard. When the people left, Elowsky got in his car to tail *them.*

When the people he thought had been snooping around his house stopped their car a short distance away, Elowsky stopped his own car and approached the other vehicle with an aluminum baseball bat, according to the occupants of the car. The two men in the car, both Boulder businessmen, said Elowsky raised the bat as if to smash the passenger side window, while yelling, "Get the [expletive] out of here."

After this, matters became even more confused. Elowsky told police one of the men in the car picked up a pipe; somehow, the television sound technician arrived on the scene. The technician told the police that Elowsky then came after him with the aluminum bat, which prompted the soundman to run away.

When police arrived to sort all this out, they arrested Elowsky on charges of felony menacing and carrying a concealed weapon—a loaded nine millimeter pistol. Elowsky was released after posting $2,500 in bail Monday afternoon.

The *Post* and the *News* both published Elowsky's address; if the Ramseys were there, those acts alone were likely to force yet another move by the embattled couple.

AN ASSESSMENT

W hen one backed away from all the media-driven frenzy, all the blind quotes from unnamed sources, all the sticks and stones thrust at the Boulder Police Department; put aside all the photographs of the smiling, dancing, singing JonBenét; cast off all the discussion about beauty pageants and anonymous letter writers, what was left?

JonBenét Ramsey was dead, and some person killed her. And despite all the distractions, the outlines of what had happened were fairly clear.

One of those who saw those outlines was Robert Ressler, John Douglas's former colleague at the FBI. Ressler came to Boulder as a consultant for a television show, *American Journal*. He went over the exterior of the crime scene, thought about the situation, and drew some fairly hard conclusions. Later, in an interview for this book, he shared them.

His first move on coming to Boulder, Ressler said, was to visit the house in daylight. In that, Ressler wasn't much different from the hundreds of people who drove or walked by the Ramsey house just to see what it looked like. The difference was, Ressler knew what to look for. Later, he returned to the house at night. He wanted, Ressler said, to "see it through the killer's eyes."

"I go out there during the nighttime," Ressler said, "and I kind of prowl around the house, hoping to hell that the cops don't come and get me. And I try to get the perspective on what the killer may have seen in the nighttime hours. Because this happened allegedly between—the word is, the kid was put to bed somewhere around eight-thirty, somewhere in there. And the parents went to bed later.

"The mother finds the note at five-thirty A.M. So there's only a window of maybe five or six hours where the killer could've gotten hold of this kid."

That meant that an outside killer had only a few hours to get inside the house, kill Jon-Benét, then write the ransom notes. The first objective of Ressler's nighttime foray was to discern whether the house could have been broken into.

"Seeing the house in the daytime indicated it was a pretty secure area," Ressler said. "You can certainly get into it, but at the same time there's stickers on the door indicating that the house was alarmed; and there was floodlighting under the eaves, and if some of them were on, it would really illuminate the exterior of the house, and it would be kind of high-risk to try to break in.

"It seemed to be a fairly substantial house, and from the standpoint of the information I had, which came largely from the media, there was no reported break-in, no forced entry. I saw some vulnerable places where a person might get in. In the back of the house there was a basement window, an opening in the ground going down, and then a basement window. This was an open trench that led to the basement window, and the well was about two feet out and four feet across, right in front of this window, and the windows were boarded up with plywood. Which would indicate that maybe they were broken at one time.

"Again there's so much missing information; whether or not somebody kicked in those windows and went in, that would take you into the basement."

Was the plywood new?

"It didn't look too old to me," Ressler said. "So that was a question: Was there a break-in? Everything I heard was there was no reported break-in. If in fact there was one, that would have been the place to go in."

Had there been a break-in at some time prior to the murder?

"Exactly," said Ressler. "And these are the

things you just don't know. The garage had a side door with glass, and that would've been an easy way to get in, too. But there was no breakage.

"So, anyway, I walked around in the nighttime and nobody's home, so I felt pretty free in doing this, and one thing I noticed in the backyard was that there was a play platform, a child's play platform built up against the tree. It was built up so you could get up into the tree. There were actually toys up in the tree. Which would indicate that kids were climbing up and down in this tree. I went up the tree, and I noticed that it looked right into a room that appeared to be either the child's bedroom, or a playroom.

"It occurred to me that a neighbor kid, who would very likely be the kind of suspect in this type of crime, could have been up in that tree and watching this child, possibly sexually curious, and maybe having an interest in the child in that fashion. Now, I didn't get into the house, there was nobody home, they probably wouldn't have let me in anyhow. I did get the impression that the house was fairly substantial, fairly secure, and if in fact people were home, a person couldn't just break in and have the freedom to walk all over the house." Someone, Ressler said, would have been likely to have discovered an intruder.

Did the murder occur in the bedroom or somewhere else in the house?

"I've seen cases," Ressler said, "I've seen a

number of cases where, in fact, a kid is killed right in the bed. A very old case comes to mind, it goes back to Chicago in the forties. William Heirens. Heirens actually went up the ladder into a bedroom window and strangled a child to death in her bed, a six-year-old child, just like JonBenét. And the parents were in the next room, and they heard the noise, and they called out in the nighttime, 'Are you all right?', they didn't hear anything, so they figured it was some sort of dream or something. And while they were crying out to the child, this guy had his hands around her throat and was killing her.

"And then he wrapped the body up in a blanket, went down the ladder—I interviewed this guy—down the ladder with her, and he sexually assaulted her and then dismembered her body after she was dead. And then he got this pang of conscience. He wrote a note, saying get $2,000 together and wait and don't call the police or the FBI, I'll be in touch. And then he went back to the house, back up the ladder, and threw the note in through the window onto the floor. So there are some similarities with this case.

"The question in this case is, essentially, was the child killed in her bed? Did the killer go into the house, did he go up the stairs, did he strangle the child in her bed, and then carry her downstairs? Or, did he pick the child up—you can pick up sleeping kids pretty easy—did he pick the kid up and carry the kid downstairs?

Did the kid become alarmed and did she start making noise, and did he shut her up by strangling her?

"In my knowledge, and the way I've seen these cases go down, if there's head damage, head injury, that came first. I think that that would come first. It doesn't make any sense to strangle somebody and then to bash their head in. Of course, under emotion people do strange things, but at the same time, I'll bet you anything when you get to the autopsy when it's done, you're going to find manual strangulation, cause of death possible head blow and manual strangulation. And the garotte and the tape was done afterward to cover up the original aspects of the crime. I don't see a person whacking this kid in the head, and then taking this elaborate garotte type instrument, wrapping it around her neck.

"I'll tell you, a garotte is a very lethal weapon, when applied properly, a garotte is something that will inflict quick and silent death. It's like using an elephant gun on a damn mouse. It's a tremendous amount of overkill. And in the taking of a small child, if we go the scenario that he got her down in the basement and started messing with her, sexually or whatever, if he's going to kill her, he's not going to get out a stick and a rope, and put it around her neck and start twisting.

"That's used when you have a difficult person to control. John Wayne Gacy, who killed thirty-three kids, used a garotte on most of his victims, who were big, strapping adolescent kids. A little child like that, it would just be crazy to stick that thing around her neck and start cranking it down. I mean, more logically, you would just manually strangle her, and hold her mouth. You wouldn't have to wrap tape around her mouth."

So what was the purpose of the tape and the garotte, if they weren't necessary?

"This whole thing was done," Ressler said, "in my opinion, as a cover. To cover up the true dynamics of what occurred in that crime. If the head blow didn't get her, then I think the manual strangulation that followed did."

But why, if having fractured JonBenét's skull and then strangled her by hand, why spend the time and effort to set up the duct tape and garotte?

"My thought is that the duct tape and the garotte, and the wrapping of the rope around the wrist, was all an attempt to make it look like some sort of bizarre murder, to cover up the truth of what really happened to the child."

All of these things happened *after* the child died, then?

"Exactly," said Ressler. "And the writing of the kidnap note. I mean, I cannot imagine, if you accept the premise that this is an attempted, aborted kidnapping, where a guy goes into the house without a kidnap note, gets the kid out of her bed, then instead of taking her out of the house, getting the hell out of there, because it's a kidnapping, okay?, he takes her to the basement, messes around with her, ends up killing her, and then after killing her, gets a notepad from the house, and nobody has ever said where that pad came from, from the upper levels or the basement, and then he sits around and makes a practice note, then makes a second note, three pages long. You know kidnap notes are by their very nature random and quick and short. And then the guy is sitting around. I mean, this is great risk, after he's killed a child, to sit there, and now compose ransom notes. If you have a ransom note, there shouldn't be a kid there. If you have a kid there, you shouldn't have a ransom note. When you have both a kid and a ransom note, it's just totally, totally bizarre and bogus, a bogus situation. The ransom note, the garotte, the rope, the tape on the mouth and neck, all that is an attempt to set up a smokescreen between the killer, his motivation, and the police."

So the duct tape was already in the house before the murder?

"The tape came from the house, like everything else," Ressler said. "I can't imagine a guy running around with a roll of tape in his pocket and not bringing material to write a note. The whole thing is just a staged event."

Well, with all the evidence, why's it taking so long for the police to make an arrest?

"What's taking so long," said Ressler, "is that the police, number one, are a small-town police department, and only have one or two homicides a year. They're not particularly skilled in homicide investigation. And then on top of that you have a wealthy family that's hired their whole investigation team to include two attorneys, one for each member of the family, a public relations guy, a psychological profiler, two investigators. In other words, they have thrown up a tremendous barrier . . .

"One of the first things you do in a case like that is interview the family. And polygraph them. John Douglas went on national television and said he'd recommended that the family not take the polygraph and not consent to interviews. I think it's ludicrous. What you've got is an ex-FBI guy who has no business in the investigation, who's jumping in . . ."

What about Chief Koby's policy toward keeping all the information about the case confidential?

"A lot of it has to be that way," said Ressler. "But then again, what's he doing with the information?"

The ransom notes: what do these indicate, if anything?

"The content of the ransom note is interesting," said Ressler. "By their very nature they're usually brief. Here they've got a rambling three-pager filled with references to a strange figure,

$118,000, which, given the parents' wealth would be like asking for $75 from somebody normal. There are the references to the father's military career, Subic Bay. I think the note is designed to make it look like somebody has got some vendetta against the family, which is what Douglas said. That's goofy. A person is going to come in like that, to get even with the family, and then leave psycholinguistic clues in the note that would link him to the family? If it's just getting even with the family, why would you leave a note?

"At the same time, let's say [the killer] did come in to kidnap the child, and killed the child accidentally. What? Are you going to write a three-page note to again provide the police with more psycholinguistic clues that wouldn't be there at all if he didn't write a note? After the child's dead, why are you writing the note? I mean, what kind of nonsense is that?

"If it were an aborted or attempted kidnapping, none of those things would have taken place. It's very clearly a cover-up type thing on somebody's part."

What about the search warrant? Why didn't the police begin their search as soon as they had the warrant, rather than telling John Ramsey to make the search himself?

"They had to get a search warrant to search the house?" Ressler asked. "To search the family's residence, the victim's residence? It's ridiculous. You [normally] don't need that, in the victim's residence, because you [usually] have consent. If you have consent to search you don't need a warrant. I mean, that's even for a suspect, let alone the victim."

If John Ramsey or anyone else told the police, Ressler said, " 'Get a warrant,' and this is allegedly a child missing, and they want to preserve her life, why would they then set up a delay tactic, which is going to slow down the police investigation during the crucial hours, when in fact the child's life might be saved? And the mere fact that the police allow non-family members to be running around the house to include escorting Ramsey on the search indicates that the police are just inept. I mean, what you normally do is get everyone the hell out of there except the immediate family."

Why didn't the police accompany John Ramsey on the search?

"Why do they even take Ramsey?" Ressler asked. "The concept that Ramsey is controlling this thing from the very onset to the extent that he apparently had, and on top of that, gets himself a dream team, as they call them, to more or less run this investigation, indicates that the police have very little control and that Ramsey has. I mean, the normal person who has had a child murdered or missing is going to be the most cooperative person in the world, because they want this case solved . . .

"There's no family member who would be beyond suspicion. Police must clear them before
they can go beyond the family and get on to more
realistic suspects. They've never been able to do
that here."

So if the death was caused by the initial blow
to the head, perhaps followed by manual strangulation, then the staging, with the rope and the
tape and garotte and the sexual assault, followed by the ransom notes, all as a cover-up to
conceal the motive of the original crime—or
even accident—all of this must have taken a
substantial amount of time.

"If in fact that child was killed intentionally or
accidentally, a person who was not [very familiar with the house] would've been out of there
as soon as they could," Ressler said. "I'm not
saying who did it, what I'm saying is, who didn't
do it.

"Who didn't do it was a casual burglar. Not a
serial killer, not a child offender, not a pedo-
phile. It was not somebody . . . who's trying to
harass or extort the family. It's an inside job.
When I say inside, it could be someone from
right around the neighborhood, people who had
access to the family. . . .

"The bottom line is that the child wasn't the
target of any type of a kidnapping," Ressler said.
"All that was staging to conceal the realities of
what happened that night, to throw up a brick
wall between the killer and the investigation."

In this, Ressler was challenging the conclusion of his former FBI colleague, John Douglas, who had told the world that the killer was likely to be an employee or former employee of Access Graphics.

MORE BRICK WALLS

The killer wasn't the only one building a brick wall; by the weekend of February 8–9, even before Jay Elowsky's arrest, the news media was becoming more and more agitated about the information barricade erected by the police.

In "Rumor Mill Runs Amok in Slaying," the *Camera*'s Krupski noted that in the absence of facts, imaginations had begun to take over. She noted the erroneous reports about the supposed confession, about the never-contemplated exhumation, along with another rumor that an unnamed Ramsey family member had committed suicide as a result of the murder.

Given that news media outlets are supposed to report facts, not rumors, Krupski's reiteration of the unsubstantiated may seem a bit odd. If it wasn't true, why legitimize it by reporting it at all? But such are the circumstances created by modern means of mass communication, where information mixes easily with gossip and speculation, and is often instantly disseminated. Reporters may wring their hands and agonize about whether to report something that's already been shown to be false. Unfortunately, they often conclude that the rumor, even if it's already been shot down, has now become part of the story . . . and so should be reported, along with the fact that it never actually happened. "It's out there," editors say, so reporters shrug and include it.

Krupski turned then to a rumor expert she identified as a social psychology professor at Tulane University, Dr. Fredrick Koenig.

"A rumor is an unverified message," Koenig told Krupski according to her report, "and it generates in the absence of any kind of credible news. When people are faced with ambiguous events where they have a hard time understanding what the causes were and who was involved, they fill things in to give events structure and make it more meaningful. We need structure so we feel comfortable."

The *News*'s Brennan weighed in as well, complaining that the "bright light of public scrutiny surrounding the JonBenét Ramsey murder investigation is being funneled into a black hole of unusual official secrecy."

As a result, Brennan observed, the public had so far been served with "a dribble of official information and a flood of rumor." Brennan enlisted a Denver journalism professor, James J.

Brodell, as an expert, which to some seemed a bit like asking the choir director to justify the choir.

"The police are our agents," Brodell said according to Brennan. "Ultimately, who is responsible for solving this crime? It's the people of Boulder, the taxpayers."

Brodell's theory of participatory democracy notwithstanding, the people actually responsible for solving the crime were the Boulder Police. "Ultimately"—to use Brodell's word—if the Boulder Police failed to apprehend the killer, it might fall to the "people of Boulder" to replace the police department or its leadership for the failure. But in the meantime the citizens of Boulder had hired the police to do the job, and if in the best judgment of the police it seemed necessary to keep information about the crime secret, one could hardly fault the police for trying to do the job they'd been hired to do.

The key question was—when? How much patience should the public be prepared to extend to the police before demanding to know what had or had not been done, and what, if anything, had gone wrong? The news media wanted this sooner rather than later; what wasn't so clear was whether the public agreed with the newspeople or—for now—the police.

On the other hand, the police reticence was creating exactly the sort of conditions that Professor Koenig had described: In the absence of hard facts, the supermarket tabloids were going wild all over again. In "Bizarre Secret Life of JonBenét's Father," the *Star* suggested that John had a secret sex life. Using a series of questions, and claiming that John had made frequent visits to Amsterdam, the tabloid made it seem like John was some sort of international pervert. Meanwhile, the *Globe* turned up some "shocking new police evidence," JonBenét's last words: "I'm going to tell Mommy." One had to buy the tabloid and read the fine print to discover that the supposed "last words" were actually those of a "source close to the case," who was imagining a "scenario."

After an unrelenting barrage of such unsubstantiated smears, the efforts of the Ramseys to keep out of sight seemed entirely understandable. But, as Koenig had pointed out, the absence of hard facts was volatile fuel to the rumor engine.

The day after Elowsky had his run-in with the purported trespassers he believed were media people, the news media went back to court in a new effort to get some of the desperately wished-for facts. The autopsy report on JonBenét had been completed by Dr. Meyer, the coroner, and the media wanted to see it, the protestations of Meyer, Koby, and Hunter notwithstanding. Boulder County District Court Judge Carol Glowinsky heard arguments from the media lawyer, Tom Kelley, and two others, representing the *Post*, the *Camera*, CBS, NBC, and several other news outlets.

Kelley told the judge that much of the information that was presumably in the autopsy report had already been leaked, and that its release would only confirm information already in the public domain. The claim by Boulder County officials that release of the information would harm the investigation had to be supported by more than just a simple assertion that harm would, in fact, result, Kelley contended. The problem with the officials' claim, he said, is that it could be applied to any murder case which was still under investigation.

But county officials were prepared for Kelley's argument. They provided the report, an addendum to the report prepared by the District Attorney's office, and two affidavits by investigating detectives, Tom Wickman and Thomas Trujillo, setting forth reasons the court should keep the autopsy sealed. The new documents were ordered sealed by the judge as well.

That, of course, made it difficult for Kelley and the other media lawyers to argue against the sealing, because without knowing what was in the new documents, they wouldn't be able to cross-examine anyone to see if sealing was really necessary.

The judge then offered Kelley a chance to look at the new documents in private if he promised not to tell anyone about their contents. This Kelley declined to consider.

"The problem is that it's hard enough to explain why I lost a case when everything happens in open court," Kelley said. "How can they [his clients] be expected to accept a result when I can't explain it to them?"

The secrecy demands of the authorities, Kelley said, seemed to be excessive—almost "Masonic."

The judge indicated she tended to be persuaded by the county's demands that the report be kept under wraps, but that she wanted to consider the arguments before making a ruling.

While all this was going on, other reporters were discovering that while Jay Elowsky was being arrested for flourishing his baseball bat, Patsy had complained to the Boulder County Sheriff's Department that the news media was harassing her and her family, which could hardly have come as news to the authorities.

The complaint, it appeared, had been lodged just before Elowsky had chased after the two men he said he'd seen in his backyard on the prior Monday. Patsy told the Sheriff's Department that Elowsky's house was surrounded by news-media types who were busy pointing telephoto lenses through the windows of the Elowsky house in order to get shots of her, Burke, and John. The street in front of the house was packed with news-media vehicles, she complained.

After Elowsky was arrested that afternoon, Patsy went to the District Attorney's office to impart her complaints to Sheriffs' investigators directly. She was accompanied by her lawyer. The visit to the Sheriff's Department raised more criticism of Patsy and the police alike. If the police were having such a problem scheduling a formal, separate interview with each of the Ramseys, and in a law enforcement setting, as had been claimed, why didn't they ask their questions when Patsy came in to the District Attorney's office to complain about the media?

It seemed entirely unfair. First her six-year-old daughter had been murdered; then lawyers had instructed her to refrain from consenting to a formal police interview, for whatever reason; then the news media had reported insinuations that she or her husband were either responsible for the death, or knew something sinister about it; then the same media had staked her out, to the point of peering at her every movement with binoculars and telephoto lenses. Then, when she complained about the harassment, she was criticized for doing what her lawyers insisted that she do. It was, in every sense promised by the putative kidnapper, a rigorous ordeal.

That night, the *Post*'s Chuck Green appeared as a guest on a popular Denver talk radio show hosted by Peter Boyles. Both Green and Boyles had been frequent critics of the Boulder police, and occasionally, the Ramseys themselves. Joining the show was Pat Korten, the Ramsey spokesman. In an interview that lasted more than two hours, Korten tried to spin the public image of John and Patsy back to where it had been before the tabloids had done their worst.

Korten said he sometimes read the worst of the tabloid headlines to John and Patsy. So far, he said, the Ramseys were standing upright against the onslaught.

"They are so numbed by the whole thing," Korten said, "that another tabloid story just doesn't mean that much anymore. It's like standing out in the cold, with the temperature at minus fifteen. When it gets down to minus twenty, it doesn't make that much difference."

Korten told Green and Boyles that the Ramsey team had provided several investigative leads on the case to the police. But, Korten said, the police didn't seem to be taking the leads very seriously. The Ramseys, Korten said, believed the police considered them the prime suspects in JonBenét's murder.

And as for the tabloid reports that the Ramsey marriage was under severe strain, Korten only scoffed.

"I wish my marriage was as close as theirs," Korten said, doubtless endearing himself to John and Patsy, if not his own wife.

DAVID AND GOLIATH

As a result of the increasingly pesky news media, District Attorney Hunter and Chief Koby held a news conference the following day, Thursday, February 13.

The bespectacled Hunter approached the podium and adopted a mien that suggested a lugubriously sorrowful Presbyterian minister determined to sermonize on his parishioners' sins without offending anyone in the congregation, his tone suggesting that it pained him to talk about such matters, but . . .

After glancing around the room to establish the appropriate gravity, Hunter gripped the podium firmly and began.

"As I watched the dawn arrive this morning I was doing my workout, which you don't allow me to do anymore at midday," Hunter said. "And I had the local paper and the two Denver papers to see what transpired about this case overnight. And it was interesting to me to read in my local paper what a reporter referred to as botched handwriting analysis, or gathering, and to peek at the Denver papers and read about what one lawyer referred to as the 'scorched earth policy' that was underway in Boulder in terms of the release of information and secrecy, and specifically with respect to the autopsy . . .

"And I thought about the responsibilities that I have, and Chief Koby has, and frankly I thought about the responsibilities that you as journalists have. I'm not a journalist, I never have been, but for almost twenty-five years I have met with many of you, and we've talked about your responsibility. You've explained things to me that I think have helped me to understand what you have to do, and what role the media plays in American society. And, in fact, I have to tell you that some of the reporting that I have reviewed has provided insights in terms of this case. And that's been true for me over the years.

"But," Hunter continued, raising his right hand to make his point, "you know, as I watched our beautiful morning come in here in Colorado, I also remembered conversations that I've had with many of you individually, about what I think is a shared responsibility in this case. And that is to do justice for JonBenét."

"It is clear to me," Hunter continued, "that these have been difficult times for you guys." Reporters, he said, had editors that pushed them hard to get more facts. But his job, and Koby's job, was to pursue the investigation with integrity.

"That means we don't want to prejudice this case," Hunter said. "We don't want to see happen to this case what I have seen happen to big cases here in Boulder, Sam Sheppard . . . and problems that you all are aware of, as journalists, that have impacted the community, the public interest over time. We don't want that to happen.

"But we know that keeping it so close to our vest has made your work very difficult, has made it tedious, has frustrated you, has resulted in part in small leaks becoming big pieces of news that have taken the front page from time to time . . . that probably is not accurate in terms of where we are going and what we are thinking about. We don't like making your jobs more difficult, because that probably comes back to get us. You guys have the barrel of ink, we have none. But I know enough of you to know we are all zeroing in on the same thing, that we are looking for the truth and we are going to do justice in this case and that's what Chief Koby and I are going to continue to do, and we hope you will understand that when we say things, we're trying to think about what we're going to say, and its impact on the viability of this case.

"We've moved to a little different stage, we feel, in this case, this investigation," Hunter continued. "Things have narrowed for us, and we think we are now at a point where we can begin to have more conversation with you, but within that framework I have just mentioned and that I spoke to you when we had the press conference in the *Globe* matters."

Hunter now made another oblique reference to the O.J. Simpson case.

"The challenge for an old prosecutor like me, given the cases that we have watched recently, is to do it right, not to use tricks, to seek out the best of the best to work on this case. Because this is not Tom Koby and Alex Hunter's case. This is a case of the people of Boulder, the people of Colorado, and certainly, without exaggeration, the people across this country who this case has touched and who call me, and I can tell when they call me they are full of emotion, that tears are often on their cheeks as they talk about the loss of this child, who was really our child.

"And that is driving us to stay on this path, a path that we hope will have as few mistakes as possible, that will be a path of truth, of high integrity, of meeting the challenge of doing it like it has not been done in a lot of cases that you and I have studied, that we have seen fail, cases that we have seen brought too quickly, including right here in Colorado, too quick a rush to judgment. We're not going to do that."

Hunter said he had a feeling about the JonBenét murder.

"I need to say to you about this case that after

a number of years, a quarter of a century . . . you come to have a feeling in your belly. You feel your instincts sort of rise to a level, it's sort of like, maybe being in a zone. That's where he [Koby] is and I am. We know where we're headed, we know this case is going to be solved. We know it."

He understood those who kept clamoring for a quick result, Hunter added.

"I get these telephone calls at all times of the day and night: Why is this thing taking so [long]? Why haven't you made an arrest? Why aren't you doing this?"

Hunter tried to indicate that the criticisms didn't bother him, but it was clear that some of the experts quoted in the news media had gotten under his skin, especially remarks that seemed to suggest that Hunter and Koby were being arrogant in denying the public information about the murder.

"Maybe it comes off as arrogance," Hunter said, apologizing if that's the way it seemed. "Tom Koby and I know who we're accountable to. We don't know everything, but we do know who we're accountable to."

Next, Hunter turned to the case itself, and attempted to offer an answer to the now-classic question of why it was taking so long.

"This is a circumstantial evidence case," Hunter said. "Those cases take longer. They require more patience, and I hope that for your viewers and your readers you will talk about the difference between some kind of eyewitness case and this kind of case that we have been dealing with, the death of this sweet, innocent, beautiful child.

"Now, I've had the feeling in recent days that you've had us on kind of a countdown atmosphere. That there's a deadline fast approaching. I have to reject that and tell you and tell your viewers that we can't be pushed into that kind of trap or fall prey to that.

"You know," he went on, "I myself feel the agony of this case every time I see a television report, read an article, see a magazine cover with the baby on it. I'd do about anything to have a rapid resolution of this tragedy. But I've got to stay on the path I've mentioned to you . . . we need to double dot the i's and double cross the t's.

"The fact that I've been in office so long, maybe too long, has allowed a continuity . . . that is probably unlike the continuity that any DA's office can boast. But I want to make it clear to you that we are not going to rest on that alone . . . [because] I've read about the composition of this team [Hunter and Koby], and you know, there's sort of a sense of, almost a David and Goliath thing . . ."

At that point Hunter dropped his first bit of real news: The authorities in Boulder had hired crime scene analyst Dr. Henry Lee—the very same criminalist who had appeared as a witness for O.J. Simpson. Nor was that all:

The Boulder officials had also retained the
services of another veteran of the Simpson defense, DNA expert lawyer Barry Scheck. In addition, Hunter said, his office had been in
contact with four other Colorado district attorneys with substantial experience in murder
cases, who had been formed into an Expert
Prosecution Task Force.

And, said Hunter, his office had reached an
arrangement with another familiar name from
the O.J. case: Cellmark Laboratories, the pres-
tigious Maryland DNA testing facility. The biological evidence that had been tested by the
Colorado Bureau of Investigation would now go
to the Cellmark people for even more testing.
That, Hunter said, was expected to take as long
as six weeks. But, he said, the authorities were
committed to doing every test necessary before
making any arrest.

"We feel," Hunter said, "that we can match the
resources of anyone, in bringing to bear on this
case, in our search for the truth to do justice,
the very best that is available."

After a few more remarks, Hunter moved to
his summary, and this time looked directly into
the camera.

"Finally I want to say to you, through you, I
want to say something to the person or persons
[who] committed this crime—the person or persons who took this baby from us. I mentioned
that the list of suspects narrows. Soon there will
be no one on the list but you.

"When that time comes and, as I have said to you, that time will come, Chief Koby and I and our people and the Expert Prosecution Task Force and the other resources that we bring together are going to bear down on you. You have stripped us of any mercy that we might have had in the beginning of this investigation. We will see that justice is served in this case, and that you pay for what you did, and we have no doubt that will happen.

"You need to know that everyone in America is watching. The death of this child has broken all of our hearts except, apparently, yours. There must be accountability, there's going to be accountability in this case, I promise you. That's my job, to make that prosecution happen, and I say to you, that there will not be any failure in that regard. We will ensure that justice is served for this community, for this nation, and most importantly, for JonBenét."

There was an almost electric atmosphere in the room after Hunter's remarks. Hunter's one-to-one challenge to the killer had focused everyone's attention on his words.

What did Hunter mean? A few odd phrases clicked into place. "We feel we can match the resources of anyone . . ." Did this mean Hunter was speaking of the wealthy Ramseys—a reference to the lawyers and public relations men hired by John and Patsy?

"You come to have a feeling in your belly . . ." Wasn't Hunter saying he knew who did it?

"You have stripped us of any mercy that we might have had at the beginning of this investigation . . ." Well, why and to whom might Hunter have felt mercy "at the beginning of this investigation?" Why mercy at all? The only mercy anyone might feel after the murder of JonBenét was for John and Patsy . . . wasn't that right?

And most of all there was the reference to David and Goliath.

It took a reporter no time at all to ask the pregnant question:

"Who's Goliath? And why would you use that analogy?"

Hunter backpedaled furiously, in the process drawing on the Simpson case as a comparison, which did little good once one recalled that the Simpson defense was the product of a wealthy defendant . . .

The reporter persisted, trying to get Hunter to name names.

"Who is Goliath? Who's your opposition and may I be more specific—"

"Obviously," Hunter said, "there is no formal opposition, and I think I've spoken sufficiently to your question . . ."

And as for the retention of Dr. Lee and Barry Scheck, reporters drew the obvious implication: that the JonBenét murder case would rival the O.J. Simpson case in intensity, and that this time, the lawmen had jumped first to get the experts as some sort of preemptive strike.

And who might have had the resources to get the Simpson experts if Hunter hadn't? The answer seemed clear to those who wanted to conjecture.

THE AUTOPSY

In the wake of Hunter's "we will get you" press conference, new attention was focused on the questions swirling around JonBenét's autopsy. Had she really been sexually assaulted? What did the medical evidence show, and what did it suggest about the perpetrator?

On the day after Hunter's promise, Judge Glowiniski ruled that some portions of the autopsy report should be made public. The released portions of the report, while not answering critical questions about the time of death, or directly, the issue of sexual assault, were nevertheless illuminating in other respects.

Under "final diagnosis," Coroner Meyer reported two broad causes of death: "ligature strangulation"—the garrote, leading to asphyxiation—and secondarily, "craniocerebral injuries"; in other words, the blunt-force trauma to JonBenét's brain. Under both categories, the redacted report deleted several listed subsections, leaving the reporters and public to guess as to what had been eliminated from public scrutiny.

What this meant was that JonBenét died from the cord around her neck. But the report also indicated that JonBenét suffered a second likely fatal injury—the hit to the side of her skull—before the strangling, exactly as Brennan had first reported, and as Ressler had suggested.

The implications of this sequence were enormously significant—yet they were little understood at this time, at least by the hordes of media attendant to the events, most of which had little knowledge of the sort of medical terminology associated with an autopsy report. Some of the brighter reporters took the redacted report to expert pathologists, but even then, most failed to ask the right questions.

As first Brennan, and then Ressler, suggested, the sequence of the injuries was critical to understanding what had transpired on that cold Christmas night. Meyer's report showed that there was substantial intercranial bleeding after JonBenét had been hit in the head—bleeding that could not have taken place after her heart was stopped by the act of asphyxiation.

Under the subheading "Brain," Meyer reported that "sections from the areas of contusion disclose disrupted blood vessels of the cortex with surrounding hemorrhage. Subarachnoid hemorrhage is also identified." The use of the word "areas" describing the injury appeared to indicate that at least two blows had been struck.

These findings strongly suggested that the events had begun with a blow or blows to the head, followed by the strangling some minutes later. In turn, this sequence suggested that Dr. Wecht's initial scenario of "a sex game gone wrong" was unlikely. What sort of a child rapist would fashion a noose first, follow it with several near-fatal blows to the head, then a tightening of the noose to induce asphyxiation? What was the sexual component in this? Even more, it seemed to show that the kidnapping-gone-wrong scenario was also highly unlikely, as Ressler had guessed.

It was possible to argue that the head injuries occurred as a kidnapper was attempting to remove JonBenét from the house. But why would a kidnapper halt his escape in order to fashion the ligature—which surely took some minutes—and then take additional time to strangle the child? And why leave the child's body behind at all, if kidnapping were the motive?

This was why Assistant District Attorney Bill Wise had said, almost from the beginning, that things about the case weren't "adding up."

There was one scenario that appeared to make a sort of sense, however, and one that was at least partially consistent with a substantial number of child homicides in the United States: that JonBenét had been struck in an angry burst of rage in the course of an argument, or possibly, slammed into a hard, stationary object such as a doorframe, a bathtub or toilet, or a piece of wooden furniture.

But why the ligature, the "garrote?" Under this hypothesis, the person or persons who caused the head injury might have panicked. Thinking the child was dead, the perpetrator or perhaps an accomplice might have removed JonBenét from the scene of the violent encounter, then fashioned the cord with the stick and tightened it in order to make the crime appear to be a kidnapping gone wrong: the so-called "staging" that all the experts seemed to agree had taken place. In this scenario, the strangling might have been an unwitting albeit gruesome accident, committed in the desperate effort to distract from the earlier violence.

Evidence for this hypothesis depended, to some degree, on the time of death, which was not included in the redacted autopsy report. Had JonBenét been killed in the middle of the night, or later? There was one possible clue from the report: Meyer reported that JonBenét's bladder was empty. That was a possible indication that JonBenét had been awake at the time of the initial assault—that the crime had taken place either the night before, just before bedtime, or in the morning after rising. Alternatively, evidence of the passing of the urine—

either among the bedsheets or at some other location in the house, such as the basement—might be an indication of where the crime had occurred. This explained why the Boulder Police had been reported removing bedding from the house, along with pieces of the carpeting.

Most of these assessments were missed by the news media, however, as reporters endeavored to shed light on the issues of sexual assault. Those questions came in two areas: was there evidence in the autopsy that a sexual assault had occurred the night of the killing, and, second, was there any evidence of previous, long-term sexual abuse?

The redacted autopsy report wasn't particularly enlightening on the first issue, whether a sex assault had taken place the night of the killing. Meyer reported in his summary that he had found evidence of vaginal abrasion and "vascular congestion of the vaginal mucosa," and in a subsection of his report, reported "focal interstitial chronic inflammation," and along the vaginal wall near the hymen, "epithelial erosion with underlying capillary congestion." Meyer reported finding "a small number of red blood cells . . . present on the eroded surface," along with "birefringent foreign material."

Translated, this indicated that there was evidence of slight scraping just inside the opening. The "birefringent foreign material" was not further identified, although some of the ubiquitous "sources" suggested that it might be something like talcum powder, perhaps used to ameliorate itching.

For the most part, these nuances were lost in the initial reporting on the sex assault issues. The day after the redacted autopsy report was released, the *Daily Camera* headlined AUTOPSY CONFIRMS ABUSE. The paper seized on the words "chronic inflammation" and "epithelial erosion," and called upon Dr. Wecht to interpret what this meant. Wecht said chronic inflammation and epithelial erosion were evidence of ongoing sexual abuse.

"This to me is evidence of sexual abuse," Wecht told the paper. "I think any forensic gynecologist and forensic pathologist would agree with that."

The Ramsey spokesman Korten rejected this interpretation utterly.

It was his understanding, Korten said, that vaginal inflammation was not uncommon "among children of that age. There has never, ever been sexual abuse of any kind."

The Denver *Post* also reported that the autopsy had concluded that JonBenét had been sexually assaulted. But the *Rocky Mountain News* was somewhat more cautious. They discussed the report with Dr. Robert Kirschner, a nationally known forensic pathologist expert in child abuse cases. Kirschner told the paper that the "chronic inflammation" could just as likely be evidence of a slight infection.

The fact was, Kirschner told the paper, "there

is just not enough information there to say." As for the erosion of the vaginal wall, that could indicate a sexual assault, Kirschner said, perhaps by a finger or some object. A "source close to the case" then confirmed to the paper that authorities believed there was evidence of digital penetration. Left unanswered was whether the possible digital penetration was part of the events of the murder, or occurred at some prior time, or even after death—let alone who did it.

HUNTER

Hunter's dramatic press conference had the effect of bringing a great deal of outside attention on himself. It was not therefore surprising, when more substantial news was not forthcoming over the next few weeks, that the news media began to look at the district attorney's background.

Hunter had been in office since 1972. He was 60 years old, and had been married four times. He had a reputation for sometimes saying and occasionally trying off-the-wall things. Once criticized for his inaction in prosecuting a police officer who had killed a man with a knife, Hunter responded by putting the investigative files in the case in a public library for public review and comment. Criticized for too much plea bargaining—a political opponent once called him the "Monty Hall of district attorneys"—Hunter abruptly decided to end plea bargains completely. The courts were soon jammed, and Hunter abandoned the idea. On another occasion, he fired his own father-in-law as an assistant district attorney when the man complained one of Hunter's witnesses was "a hippie" and threatened to punch him.

Hunter's longevity in office could be traced in part to his abiding interest in local politics. A Democrat, Hunter was well plugged into the party's Colorado establishment, and was active in party affairs. He was aligned with the party's liberal faction, and was known to Gov. Roy Romer, the current chairman of the Democratic National Committee, and to the old Gary Hart faction of the party in Colorado. One of Hart's close associates in his aborted campaign for president in 1988 was Hal Haddon—one of the principal partners in the law firm hired by John Ramsey.

It would therefore be accurate to say that Hunter was a man who was well-schooled in the nuances of political opinion—as expressed by ordinary voters, as well as the power elite. His task would be to steer a careful course between the potential pitfalls of precipitous action in the JonBenét case, and the likely politically fatal outcome of doing nothing at all.

In an interview with the *Rocky Mountain News*'s Burt Hubbard, Hunter seemed to suggest that in getting the JonBenét Ramsey murder case, he'd been given an opportunity to demonstrate that the American criminal justice system *could* work—the verdict in the O.J. Simpson case notwithstanding.

"I feel that my responsibility is much broader than to the people of Boulder County," he told Hubbard. "The challenge in great part is to do this case right to show the public that a case's integrity can be protected."

But while Hunter had his eyes fixed on saving the American criminal justice system from its excesses, his assistant Bill Wise was criticizing the Boulder Police before the Boulder County Commissioners. Wise, standing in for Hunter, wanted the commissioners to appropriate another $150,000 to the district attorney's budget to pay for work on the investigation. In the course of his presentation, Wise commented that the Boulder Police had been uncooperative with the district attorney's office in the Jon-Benét case, and that the Boulder officers were inexperienced. One of the main problems was that the Boulder detectives, or at least some of them, resented advice being given to them by Hunter's chief trial deputy, Peter Hofstrom.

"He'd like to do a lot of it," Wise said of Hofstrom, "and the Boulder Police Department says, 'Get out of our business.' They don't like lawyers sticking their noses into their investigations and trying to run crime scenes and so forth." Wise indicated that the district attorney's office believed that the Boulder police had nearly mishandled some important forensic evidence, and that they had rebuffed offers of crime scene assistance from Denver police.

This shed some light on the "animated discussion" held between the district attorneys and the police at the house at the time of the eight-day search.

The detectives were angered by Wise's off-the-cuff remarks, not least because they soon found their way into the news media. The following day, Wise apologized to the police, as did Hunter. But it appears that some of the squabbling observed between the detectives and the district attorneys at the crime scene had taken deep root. Eventually, these problems would arise again.

For one thing, Hunter was hardly the only one in Boulder who had his eyes on the JonBenét murder case, and what it might mean for the immediate political future. Among those others were Police Chief Koby, the former Houston star who had never been universally loved by the Boulder department's rank and file; the Boulder Police Officers' Association, which was about to enter new contract negotiations with the city; City Manager Tim Honey, whose support among the members of the City Council was shaky; and Boulder Police detective commander John Eller, the man who headed the detectives criticized by Wise.

What wasn't generally known then, in Boulder, was that Eller had been looking for a new job—as a police chief. Solving a nationally famous murder case might look good on anyone's resume, and Eller had a number of resumes out even as the investigation continued.

As February turned into March, little of substance appeared to be transpiring. Hunter held another press briefing, in which he told of interviews with the 1958 Miss America, Marilyn Van Derbur Atler. Atler six years earlier had revealed that she had been a victim of sexual abuse by her father when she was a child, and was now recognized as an expert on incest. Hunter said he had his own conversations with Atler, and called her "a significant resource" in the Jon-Benét investigation.

The *Post*'s Chuck Green almost immediately took a swipe at Hunter.

"Trying to interpret Hunter's words is akin to reading tea leaves," Green complained. "He seems to be saying things—sending signals—without actually saying anything."

The public reference to Atler, suggested Green, could be Hunter's backhanded way of saying that authorities suspected incest and sexual abuse in the JonBenét case.

Green's uneasiness with Hunter's now-you-see-it, now-you-don't briefing style pointed out the contradictions posed when a politically adroit prosecutor faces intensive media scrutiny: at what point does the desire to look good—to hint at action—overcome careful management of a criminal case? If there was no evidence of ongoing sexual abuse, wasn't producing Atler as "a significant resource" in the investigation a form of grandstanding? Or was something more going on?

"What did it all add up to?" Green mused. "Virtually no solid information, but another five cords of verbal firewood to fuel even more speculation."

ELIMINATIONS

After the frenetic events of January and February, the investigation into JonBenét's death had reached a sort of lull. Things were happening, but they were not readily apparent in their significance, as if the investigation was a soup that had to simmer to achieve the proper flavoring. The general expectation was that the biological material sent to the Cellmark Laboratories might provide the definitive answer as to who killed JonBenét, and that until those results were returned there was nothing to do but wait.

Weekly press briefings in Boulder began to assume some of the characteristics of the British House of Commons's Prime Minister's Question Time as shown on C-SPAN. Spokesman Kelvin McNeil would appear before the assembled media on Thursdays, bearing a binder as if he were John Major or Tony Blair. Reporters would ask questions, McNeil would consult his binder for the appropriate response, and say what he'd already said many times before. One half-expected O'Neill to say, as the British Prime Minister traditionally does, "I refer the right honorable gentleman to the answer I gave some moments ago."

A few side trips erupted, however. In early March, the *News*'s Brennan reported that police had collected hair and handwriting samples from a woman who was married to a man who had played the role of Santa Claus at a Ramsey Christmas party given two nights before the murder.

This was Janet McReynolds, 64, the wife of Bill McReynolds, 67, a retired professor. Bill McReynolds's subject at the University of Colorado was, of all things, journalism. Mrs. McReynolds was for a decade the drama critic for the *Daily Camera*.

Brennan reported that the police wanted the samples from Mrs. McReynolds (they already had some from Mr. McReynolds) because of several peculiar coincidences.

For one thing, Brennan reported, the McReynolds' daughter, then nine years old, was abducted briefly in Longmont, Colorado, in 1974, where she saw a friend, also held, subjected to sexual molestation. The date of this event was December 26—the same day as JonBenét's kidnapping and death was discovered.

Further, Mrs. McReynolds, a poet and a playwright, had written a play titled *Hey Rube*, which centered on the sexual assault, torture and murder of a girl. In the play, the girl's body is eventually discovered in a basement.

Both McReynoldses were perfectly willing to discuss the situation with Brennan.

"I know I had absolutely nothing to do with it," Bill McReynolds told Brennan. He said he and his wife had gone to bed at 8 P.M. Christmas night. The police had told them that they wanted the samples for the purposes of excluding the McReynoldses as suspects.

"You know," McReynolds mused, "I always told my students to seek the truth. Now I'm on the other side of it [the media attention] . . . I'm probably stupid and naive."

These and other events obscured the real state of the investigation. By this time, detectives had returned to Georgia to interview other friends, relatives and former neighbors of the Ramseys; they made trips to other states as well. They returned once more to the house in Charlevoix, Michigan for another search, and began to track down the various people who had come in contact with the Ramseys in Boulder.

The objective was to identify anyone who knew the Ramsey family well enough to know the sorts of things about the Ramsey affairs as indicated in the ransom note, who also might have been able to gain access to the Ramsey home on Christmas night. There were a number of keys to the house held by outsiders, which required detectives to interview scores of others who might have had access to the keys, and to determine what these persons' alibis might be. In that regard, the police were fortunate: the fact that the crime occurred on Christmas night made it quite easy to verify these alibis. In general, the effort was, as with the McReynoldses, to exclude possibilities. The circumstances of the crime made that relatively easy: who had access to the house, knew enough about the Ramsey business and John Ramsey's personal life to write the note, and who could not account for their whereabouts on Christmas night.

As this work was going forward, however, another battle was being played out behind the scenes between the district attorney's office and the lawyers for the Ramseys. The issue of the long-awaited formal interview wasn't going away, and both sides continued to maneuver over the terms and conditions of the interview. Hunter's reference to Atler as "a significant resource" to the investigation might be interpreted as a shot across the Ramsey bow: that if the Ramseys didn't come in soon to deal with the suspicions against them, Hunter would not be able to restrain the voracious speculation of the media against them, however inaccurate it might be.

For their part, the Ramseys felt abused by both Hunter and the police. New speculation had again erupted about John Andrew's whereabouts, partly because Hunter refused to publicly confirm it, and this infuriated the Ramseys. When detectives went to Atlanta to speak again with Cindy, John's former wife, she declined to speak with them, as did the two older children. In turn, that required the detectives to independently verify the two older children's alibi.

The Ramseys' public relations man, Korten, then went public with a demand published on the Internet that the authorities clear John Andrew and Melinda once and for all.

"It should be made perfectly clear by the Boulder Police Department," the statement said, "that John Andrew is not a suspect in this horrible crime. To continue to refuse to do so is cruel to a fine young man and to the rest of our family." Four days later, McNeill, reading from his binder again, said the two older children had in fact been eliminated as suspects—the first time the police had ever declared positively that a particular person had *not* committed the crime.

But this time McNeill also had some real news to report. The Colorado Bureau of Investigation had completed its initial handwriting analyses, and had concluded that John Ramsey did not write the ransom note.

But the results on Patsy, McNeill said, were inconclusive. More samples would be needed.

In early March, the *News's* Brennan tracked down what promised to be a significant piece of information: the snow. Brennan determined that there was snow on the ground around the Ramsey house from December 16 through December 26, and that it had snowed lightly on Christmas afternoon and evening. But, said Brennan, police found no footprints around the Ramsey house.

"This is one of the earliest details that caused investigators [to focus] on the slain girl's family," Brennan reported, attributing his information to "police sources."

No footprints? What were the police doing when the Denver *Post* reported that they were busily measuring footprints around the house in the days after the body was discovered? This appears to be a case of imprecision on the part of Brennan's sources. Clearly there were footprints around the house from the friends, ministers, doctors, lawyers and police who had arrived at the house on December 26 in the wake of the discovery of the ransom note. Where on the property, then, would the absence of footprints have been suspicious?

How about around the basement window— the one that had been covered with plywood after, as it turned out, the police had discovered it standing open on the morning of the crime, and had then taken into evidence? The window so noticed by Robert Ressler?

If there was an open window to the basement, and there were no footprints in the snow around the well protecting the window, the implication was obvious: that the window had been opened by someone inside the house, possibly to make police believe that had been the method of entry. This sounded like more of the "staging."

The net effect of this report was to focus attention once more on the Ramseys, and to again bring into question their reluctance to agree to a formal interview.

Suspects

Over the next month, new details about the crime continued to emanate from "sources." The *Post*'s Marilyn Robinson reported that "although 6-year-old murder victim JonBenét Ramsey had been sexually assaulted, no semen was found at the crime scene . . ."

This served to shove the prospects of the Cellmark DNA analysis to the back of the stove. That biological material from the body had been recovered was not disputed; the significance of those recoveries, in the absence of the establishment of the sex-activity positive evidence of semen, was enormously problematical.

"Sources told the Denver *Post*," Robinson reported, that "semen was not found on or near the body, in the girl's bedroom or in the basement room where her body was found . . ."

So much for the easy solution; any semen present at any part of the crime scene would be *prima facie* evidence that the murder was a sex crime, and indicative, after DNA analysis, of the identity of the perpetrator. The absence of semen gave rise to the inference that the motive for the killing had nothing to do with sex, and was indeed related to other issues.

But still, there was the DNA evidence that had been collected: reportedly, scrapings from under JonBenét's fingernails, a "fluid" found on or near the body, possibly hairs missed by the killer who had wiped the body clean, and perhaps other components of so-called "trace" evidence. If none of these were sex-crime specific, as was semen, might they be useful in linking possible perpetrators to the scene? Perhaps, except that alternative explanations for the presence of these biological or trace materials might be easily advanced by any competent defense lawyer.

A week later, the *News*'s Brennan advanced this line. In RAMSEY SLAYING MAY NOT BE LINKED TO SEX, Brennan for the first time separated the facts of the crime from the image of the victim: in asserting that "investigators are closely examining an alternative theory," Brennan advanced the notion that JonBenét had been the victim of a "deadly physical attack . . . [not] motivated by sex, and [that] didn't include sexual abuse."

Brennan trotted out another forensic pathologist, who said he'd read the autopsy report three times, and, contrary to Dr. Wecht's "sex game" assertion, there was no evidence to support that the crime was related to any sexual assault.

"The way it reads," said Dr. Wilbur Richie, the Jefferson County, Colorado, coroner, "it in no way suggests sexual assault."

This reporting had the effect of throwing the entire case into an entirely new light. If there was no semen, if there was no sexual assault—if there was no connection to the JonBenét of the beauty pageants, the lipstick, the eye shadow, the coquettish videotapes and the still photographs; in other words, no sex—what was going on?

Just about any way anyone looked at the killing, if all this no-sex idea was true, some argued it had to come back to the Ramsey family. But was this only the shallow result of the leaks from the "sources," who might have had their own agenda, an agenda generated by their failure to identify evidence of a real, outside perpetrator?

And if so, what was that agenda? To put enough public pressure on the Ramseys—through the tabloids, through the radio talk shows, through selective leaks to Robinson or Brennan or others—to make the Ramseys finally collapse and agree to the long-sought "formal interview?"

Leakers who suggested this line also speculated that some violent, non-sexual event might have transpired at the Ramsey house the night of the murder. This scenario in turn was tantamount to suggesting that one or the other or both of the Ramseys had succumbed to some sort of fatal child abuse in the midst of a family dispute: some outpouring of rage, triggered by stresses one could only guess at, which had nothing at all to do with sexual abuse, or the darker issues of Atler's ideas about incest.

Those lurid sex components, so prominent indeed in the earlier phases of reporting on the case, could in this scenario easily be seen as only the result of the feverish imagination of the media, fixated as ever on the images of sex and violence, in order to make their increasingly market-driven products advance their venues' sales, whatever the cost to individuals, and to the truth.

All of which only added to the pressure: when, if ever, would the Ramseys come in to be interviewed? When would the Ramseys come forward to tell the police, once and for all, what really happened in their house on Christmas night?

Then Hunter cranked up the stakes once more.

"Obviously," Hunter told the Associated Press in the middle of April, "the focus is on these people."

Did Hunter mean to say that "these people"—John and Patsy—were *suspects*?

"You can call them what you want to," he said.

*　　*　　*

Hunter's decision to publicly admit the obvious—that the Ramseys were "the focus" of the investigation—seemed calculated to precipitate the long-postponed interview. It quickly drew results, although probably not the sort Hunter expected.

Lawyers for the Ramseys had been in negotiations with the police for these interviews for months. Hunter then spoke out, naming the Ramseys as the "focus" April 18, 1997. Judging from the sequence of subsequent events, it appears that Hunter's pronouncements had the desired effect: within a few days of his statement, the Ramsey side agreed to comply with the Boulder Police Department's desire for the "formal interview."

However, in retrospect, it appears that the Boulder police were so eager to have this discussion that they agreed to conditions they ordinarily should have summarily rejected—and were quickly so informed by the FBI.

All of this erupted a few days later, when the Ramsey lawyers—with Hal Haddon, the politically prominent ally of Hunter, riding point—exploded at the Boulder department, claiming that the police had reneged on an agreement governing the interview with John and Patsy.

Haddon's law firm vented considerable vitriol toward the Boulder police, blaming them for the collapse of the long-awaited interview. The Ramsey lawyers contended the police abandoned agreed-upon conditions for the interview just hours before it was to have been conducted.

In military tactics, this is known as seizing the high ground. In Haddon's view—dispatched in a letter sent to Hunter, but also disseminated to the press—John and Patsy were depicted as more than willing to cooperate in the investigation; it was the police who were not to be trusted. It soon developed that the police withdrew their offer for these interviews based upon advice from the Federal Bureau of Investigation's Behavioral Sciences Unit—Ressler and Douglas' old stomping grounds.

These aborted interviews—Patsy had been scheduled for the morning, John for the afternoon—were to have occurred at a neutral site: the offices of a Boulder lawyer agreeable to both sides. However, late in the day before the interrogations were to have taken place, someone in the Boulder Police Department called the Ramsey lawyers to cancel the discussions. The Ramsey lawyers fumed; they felt they'd been set up, first by Hunter, then by the police.

The cancellation, Haddon and Patrick Burke wrote, was "a very deliberate action by authorities who think it is more appropriate to leak information than to interrogate."

Now the long-bubbling dispute between the Ramsey team and the Boulder authorities was finally out in the open. The letter distributed by Haddon and Burke contained some incendiary language.

"This action is incomprehensible," Haddon

and Burke wrote, "in light of the previous history of this issue. The Police Department, directly and through a campaign of leaks and smears, has portrayed the Ramseys as unwilling to grant police interviews or assist the investigation.

"Although we know this innuendo to be false, we have avoided criticizing the police because we believed that it would only fuel a media war which would be counterproductive to the overarching goal—finding and prosecuting the killer of JonBenét Ramsey. Yesterday's actions make further silence untenable."

This, indeed, was a threat: that the Ramseys would cease their silence and instead go after the Boulder Police, and possibly even Hunter himself.

Haddon and Burke went on to detail their side of the negotiations over the long-awaited interviews.

"All the arrangements for these interviews had been made and agreed upon," they wrote. "John and Patsy were anxious to participate, based on Mr. Hofstrom's [Hunter's deputy] representations that such interviews would assist in apprehending the killer of their daughter. We cannot describe their anguish and disappointment when we were forced to advise them that the police had reneged on the interviews you earnestly requested on April 11."

Haddon and Burke contended that the Ramseys had offered interviews to the police as far back as January, but the police had rejected them.

Even worse, they said, the police had tried to extort an early interview from the Ramseys by trying to prevent the release of JonBenét's body in time for the funeral—in effect, holding the body as a hostage in an effort to induce cooperation. The Ramsey lawyers had to threaten to sue to get the body released.

"Since that time," they wrote, "law enforcement authorities from several agencies have launched a cowardly smear campaign against John and Patsy, fueled by leaks and smears attributable only to 'sources.' We will no longer endure these tactics in silence. It is beyond comprehension that law enforcement authorities prefer to leak information rather than interrogate the person who they characterize as 'suspects' in their investigation.

"It is apparent," Haddon and Burke's letter continued, "that the leadership of the Boulder Police Department lacks the objectivity and judgement necessary to find the killer of JonBenét Ramsey.

"Mr. Hofstrom told John and Patsy that he wanted their help to solve this crime." The Ramseys, Haddon and Burke asserted, were willing to meet with anyone, except for personnel from the Boulder Police Department, to discuss the crime.

The Ramsey offensive against the police—particularly since it was carried out behind the

weight of the politically prominent Haddon—
had the effect of putting the police on the defensive. No longer was the issue the seeming lack
of cooperation by the Ramseys, but now it was
also the honesty and credibility of the police—
right down to the unseemly squabble over
JonBenét's body.

"You can only imagine what effect that event
had on the Ramseys' confidence that this was
an objective investigation," Haddon told Charlie
Brennan. "I think that fact goes a long way toward explaining why the Ramseys have been
less than enthused about the objectivity of the
Boulder Police Department."

Stung, the police responded with their own
press release that attempted to put the onus of
the seemingly stalled investigation back on the
Ramseys. "Their reluctance to provide witness
information continues to hinder the police investigation into the murder of their daughter,"
the statement said.

What was the FBI advice to the police that
prompted the cancellation? No one would say,
except to observe that the conditions of the
agreement—neutral ground and a time limit—
were not thought to be helpful to a "productive"
interview.

Productive of what? Of admissions or evasions—the grist for any normal police interrogation of a suspect in a crime? The cardinal
principle of interviewing anyone suspected of a
crime is to maintain control of the interview. By

keeping the pressure on, by cultivating an atmosphere of subtle menace, the interrogator works to envelop the suspect in a weave of details leading to contradictions. The contradictions inevitably lead to lies and evasions, and the lies, provided enough psychological pressure is maintained, eventually lead to admissions and finally, confessions. In the Ramsey case, the agreement to interview first John, then Patsy—separated by several hours and a break for lunch—was not conducive to police maintaining the control they required.

If it suspected the Ramseys, just why the Boulder Department thought it could extract worthwhile information from the Ramseys at a neutral site, under time limits, and at separate times wasn't entirely clear. It may have been that detectives were so frustrated at their inability to question the Ramseys that they were willing to agree to anything. But the FBI brought the department back to reality.

The *Post*'s Chuck Green nailed this down.

In FBI SAVES PROBE FROM DISASTER, Green wrote that "It doesn't take a Sherlock Holmes to figure this one out." The separate interviews would have provided Patsy the opportunity to learn what police had asked of John; that in turn could have permitted Patsy to tailor her own responses in her interview several hours later. The proposed lunch break between the two sessions would have provided ample time, Green contended.

"Over linguine at Pasta Jays, perhaps, Ramsey and his attorneys would review all the questions police asked and all the answers Ramsey gave them. By the time gelato is served, Mrs. Ramsey would have been thoroughly briefed on the morning's session."

MUDDLING TO THE MIDDLE

The feuding between the Ramseys and the police continued over the next few days, with both sides issuing press releases that pointed the finger of blame at the other. After so many weeks of cryptic silence, the sudden burst of talk seemed to presage some sort of development. The new volubility from the Ramseys seemed as much public relations as anything else, an attempt to move the needle of public opinion back toward their own side of the dial in the wake of the increased speculation that the Ramseys were the killers.

All this ill feeling put Hunter in a difficult position: on one hand, he was the principal law enforcement officer for the county, the one person who had the power to bring any criminal charges to court, and as such, one who had to maintain a good working relationship with the police. On the other hand, there was no advantage to Hunter in offending the Ramseys and their politically influential lawyer, Haddon. As was his wont, Hunter began to look for some sort of compromise, some middle way to smooth the troubled waters.

A letter offering new conditions for the interview was sent by Hunter and Koby to the Ramsey lawyers, along with an expression of regret for the acrimony that had blown up.

"We acknowledge the unfortunate miscommunication, and we're encouraged to hear you indicate a continued willingness to accomplish the critical interviews with Mr. and Mrs. Ramsey," the letter said.

"Ultimately," the letter continued, "everyone wants the same outcome—to identify whoever committed this crime."

Hunter said he decided to publicly release this letter because the Ramsey lawyers had gone public first.

"Our press release is in response to theirs," Hunter told the *Post*. "It required an answer. And frankly, I want to take them up on their cooperative attitude. It helps to advance the investigation."

"We felt that the police department, frankly, was inaccurately portrayed in their letter," said Boulder city spokesman Leslie Aaholm. "We felt they'd gone public, so we had to go public. We are not going to necessarily continue this activity. Obviously, this was a strategic decision on their part. They shot a volley over the bow, and we've responded . . ."

While this was going on, Patsy Ramsey decided to go public, too. She called a Denver television station to declare that neither she nor her husband had anything to hide.

"I will sit with investigators around the clock if that's what they want," Patsy said. "You'd think if they believed we were guilty they'd want to talk with us."

This Patsy was such a vast departure from the tabloid image of Patsy that had so dominated the case for the previous few months that it was nearly startling. It appeared that the Ramseys were preparing to come out and fight back.

Discussions between Hunter and the Ramseys' lawyers continued over the next few days. Hunter kept trying for the middle ground.

"This investigation requires an open mind," he told the *News*'s Kevin McCullen, "and there are many other individuals who have been looked at and who are being looked at." The fact that JonBenét had been found dead in the family home where there was no sign of forced entry made the Ramseys only an "obvious" focus of an investigation, but not necessarily the only one.

Over the weekend, the negotiations continued. The Ramseys were still willing to be interviewed, it appeared, but only if the police first agreed to provide the Ramseys with copies of the statements John and Patsy had initially made to the police on December 26 and 27.

This appeared to be a hard demand, and agreeing to it would be highly unusual, if not irregular. Presumably, by reading the copies of their initial statements, John and Patsy might better prepare themselves for new police questions. After consideration, Hunter decided to agree to the demand. The statements were turned over to the Ramseys' lawyers.

"The statements by the Ramseys were meager at best," Hunter said on the following Monday, "and when the content of the reports was measured against the value of interviewing the Ramseys, it was determined that the interviews were of greater value than giving up the reports."

Hunter's decision to give up the reports was roundly criticized by other law enforcement professionals. The *Post*'s Chuck Green produced former FBI agent Gregg McCrary, who called Hunter's decision "crazy" and "bizarre."

"You just don't give suspects that kind of information," McCrary told Green. "It makes whatever interview you get invalid."

What was worse, Green opined, was that while the Ramseys got the statements, the police didn't get the interview.

"Such a deal," Green wrote.

But Green was wrong, because on the same day his column appeared, the Ramseys were being interviewed for the first time since that awful December day, a little more than four months before.

GOING PUBLIC

The interviews took place at the Boulder County district attorney's office. Patsy arrived first, shortly after 8 A.M., and was questioned by two Boulder police detectives and someone from the district attorney's office. Patsy's lawyer, Patrick Burke, and an investigator from the Ramsey team also sat in on the interrogation. The session with Patsy lasted about six and a half hours, ending about 3 P.M.

The word was out that the interview was taking place, and the news people scrambled to "stake out" the Justice Center in case something happened. Some saw John arrive at the Justice Center shortly after 3 P.M. That seemed to indicate that the FBI's advice had prevailed: that John and Patsy were interviewed separately, with perhaps no opportunity to consult with one another before John's interview. While John was being interviewed, Patsy was allowed to stay in Hunter's office. After John's interview was completed about 5:30, the Ramseys were allowed to leave the building by using an exit that wasn't under the news media's observation.

But the reporters would soon get their crack at the Ramseys as well.

The calls came at night from the Ramsey lawyers. Seven news organizations out of the scores that were covering the case were selected. Three newspapers, three television stations, and a radio station were chosen. Editors were instructed to have reporters in Boulder by 10 A.M. the following day. They were to have pager numbers where the Ramsey lawyers could reach them.

The following morning, each of the reporters got the pages from the Ramsey lawyers. Each was given a codeword, and after being sworn to secrecy, was given instructions on where to go next.

The Ramseys laid the following conditions on the selected representatives of the media: no exterior photographs of the facility where the press conference would be conducted; no questions about facts relating to the killing; no questions about what the police had asked the Ramseys the day before; no questions of the Ramsey lawyers, or even photographs of them.

Once at the secret location, the media people had to give the codeword. At that point, each news person was provided with a small, white, circular identification adhesive badge, and admitted.

Both Ramseys looked calm and collected. Patsy, in fact, was vastly improved from the shaky, grief-stricken person who had appeared on CNN in January. Dressed in a tasteful blue suit, she looked directly at the reporters and listened intently to their questions, and was clearly in control of her emotions. John was likewise in control of himself, and was even capable of displaying a sense of humor. Clearly, neither of the Ramseys was quivering with fear that they might soon be arrested, and in fact, the entire tenor of their demeanor showed they would be formidable witnesses if ever called into court.

John opened the press conference by saying that now that the police had completed their interrogation, both he and Patsy felt more free to speak than they had before.

"I think one of the issues that was distressing to us and that perhaps caused some bias of opinion is, why did we bring lawyers into the process early on," John said. "I can tell you both how that happened and why that happened."

The day JonBenét's body was discovered, John said, a family friend who was also a lawyer took him aside and suggested that because a substantial majority of child homicides in the United States are family-related, that John and Patsy should take steps to have lawyers. To do otherwise when they would be a focus of the investigation, John said, would be foolish.

Next John addressed the primary question:

"To those of you who may want to ask, let me address, very directly, I did not kill my daughter, JonBenét. There have also been innuendos that she has been or was sexually molested. I can tell you those were the most hurtful innuendos to us as a family. They are totally false. JonBenét and I had a very close relationship. I will miss her dearly for the rest of my life."

Patsy then took up the same question.

"I'm appalled that . . . either John or I could be involved in such a hideous, heinous crime. But let me assure you that I did not kill Jon-Benét, I did not have anything to do with it. I loved that child with the whole of my heart and soul."

Asked why it had taken so long to get the formal interview out of the way, and how he would respond to those who criticized them for the delay and the reported refusal to take a polygraph test, John said this was because the Ramseys both felt insulted that they might even be considered as suspects, and "felt an interrogation of ourselves was a waste of our time and a waste of the police's time." But, he added, he and Patsy finally decided it was necessary to agree to the interrogation so the police could get on with other leads.

The Ramseys went on to thank the people who had send them cards and letters of support, and called attention to a $100,000 reward the family had offered for the arrest and conviction of the killer.

"What do you want to say to the killer of your daughter?" John was asked.

"We'll find you. We will find you. I have that as the sole mission for the rest of my life," John said.

And what would Patsy say to JonBenét?

"I talk to JonBenét . . ." Patsy began, and for the first time she began to falter. "And I tell her I love her."

These twin developments, first the police interrogations, followed by the Ramseys' own public statements, appeared to fulfill two purposes for the Ramseys. For one thing, by issuing such firm denials that they had anything to do with the death of their daughter, the Ramseys were trying to swing the pendulum of public opinion back in their direction, or at least get it back to neutral. For another, the Ramseys had clearly demonstrated to any prosecutor that they would hardly be pushovers as witnesses in court.

This didn't stop the nation's usual crowd of rubbernecking laywers from rushing in to comment on the new Ramsey tactics. Even as the Ramseys were holding their press conference, CNN's *Burden of Proof* was canvassing a mix of lawyers as to whether they would have allowed the Ramseys to speak to the police under the circumstances.

Greta Van Susteren:

"Bernie. Here you have John and Patsy Ramsey, who have not been charged with anything so far, it appears that the investigation is at a standstill. They must have the DNA tests, the investigation must be near its end. Why in the world would any lawyer let the two Ramseys, who must be the focus, talk to the police?"

Bernard Grimm, criminal defense attorney:

"You ask an excellent question, Greta. No lawyer in their right mind, at this stage, would let their clients respectively talk to the police. It can only hurt their clients. It can only get their clients indicted, it can only get their clients charged. My guess is they want to maintain a certain social appearance in their community, in their social strata . . ."

Grimm compared the Ramseys' agreement to talk with the police to O.J. Simpson's decision to do the same.

"I agree with Bernie," said Van Susteren. "It was nuts to have those two talk to the police."

It seemed that there was no way for the Ramseys to make anyone happy, no matter what they did.

DEAD IN THE WATER

W as Van Susteren right? Was the investigation of the murder of JonBenét Ramsey really at a standstill? It often seemed so in the weeks ahead. For all the hope that had been pinned on the DNA evidence, the results, when they came, were said to be disappointing. For reasons that were obscure, the police declined to show the results to Hunter.

However, this appeared to be one of the results of the sometimes prickly relationship between the Boulder Police and Hunter's office. Brennan talked to sources who contended that Eller, the detectives' commander, was attempting to control everything about the investigation, and that a personality problem had blown up between the two offices. One lawyer familiar with the situation told Brennan, "They may be all in the same canoe, but they aren't rowing in the same direction."

These frictions were not the least of the troubles besetting the investigation. The police union voted no-confidence in Koby's leadership, not necessarily because of the Ramsey investigation, but still adding to the stress of the entire situation. The Boulder City Manager, Tim Honey, locked in contract negotiations with the union, defended Koby.

"Are there issues facing the police department?" Honey asked rhetorically. "Yes. Am I concerned about the department falling apart, or about Tom Koby's leadership? No."

Honey might not have been concerned about Koby, but Koby might have done better to be concerned about Honey. Within two weeks, Honey was out—the City Council bought out the remainder of his contract when it became apparent that Honey no longer had the support of the majority of the council members.

Koby went on vacation in Houston, but not before predicting that it would be months more before an arrest might be expected—if at all.

So what went wrong? How was it possible that the killing of a six-year-old girl, inside her own house on Christmas night, apparently without a shred of positive evidence to indicate the presence of an intruder, could remain unsolved?

There was ample circumstantial evidence:

As far as anyone had been able to prove, there were only four people in the Ramsey house on the night JonBenét was killed: John, Patsy, Burke, and JonBenét herself.

There was nothing anywhere in the house to indicate a forced entry, unless one counted the open window, and speculated that a bird was the break-in artist.

The evidence showed that the head injuries came first, which in turn seemed to indicate that the rest of the crime—the duct tape, the strangling, the ransom notes—were part of a coverup.

The killer seemed to be someone familiar with the floor plan of the house, and was comfortable enough inside the house to remain there for a substantial period of time, even under stress.

The writer of the ransom notes was familiar with many intimate details of John Ramsey's life and work.

All of these circumstances gave rise to inferences about the nature of the crime, and none of them excluded either John or Patsy or both from having been the participants.

But these inferences were negative arguments. Just as true was the fact that there was no positive evidence linking anyone to the crime, either.

Despite the passage of months, this practice note was not subjected to fingerprint analysis until the very end. Why? Because, the *News*'s Brennan reported, the practice note had been provided to police by John Ramsey himself on the day JonBenét's body was discovered—when investigators asked John for a sample of Patsy's handwriting. A police officer discovered the practice note while leafing through the pad. It thus appeared that Patsy had previously handled the notepad which contained the practice note, and so had John—at the very least when he brought the pad to the police in response to their request. Police later discovered, Brennan reported citing unnamed sources, that the longer ransom note came from the very same pad, a pad that had been extensively handled before the killing by one of the primary focuses of the investigation.

BETRAYAL

There is, in such situations as the murder of JonBenét Ramsey, a sense of something organic about the events, a natural evolution that is comprised of equal measures of facts, images, prognostications, and explanations. Like a sentient creature, the whole is born, then grows, reaches a maturity, and then begins to die out.

The growth of the phenomenon known as the JonBenét case was nurtured throughout by the hothouse culture of the news media; and, like every other similar event that binds us into a shared if illusional common experience, the natural conclusion for the JonBenét event was the expectation of an arrest. That way the story could die, as expected, to be replaced by something else.

But what if it never happened? What if, like TWA Flight 800, the event just petered out without any finality? What if it passed into history as a momentary aberration, just another side-show along the midway of the American century? In the end, the networks would pack their cameras off to some new locale, the daily stories in the newspapers would dwindle, the tabloids would go screaming off after something else. The police would plod along, weighing possibilities, but making no real progress, and the death of JonBenét would pass into history, receding ever farther from our awareness. In the coming years, when we thought of JonBenét Ramsey at all—if we ever would—we would remember her as we had always seen her: all dressed up with no place to go.

And there was a tragedy: that we would remember JonBenét not for who she was, for we never really knew her, but only as she had been portrayed.

That other JonBenét, the one we never knew: a little girl, innocent if precocious, who loved her puppy, who considered her daddy the best man in the world, a kindergartener who knew nothing of the sordid preoccupations of the world of adults, who lived her short life with joy and unbounded happiness, who was robbed of her humanity and dignity and birthright in a single night's terror. And it was the horror of this act, perpetrated on an innocent six-year-old, that held us in thrall. How could there be such evil? And we told ourselves that it wasn't right, and that justice must be done. When it wasn't forthcoming, we felt betrayed by our illusions.

Where have the authorities gone wrong? The grim answers are in the evident lack of police training and experience that allowed so many errors on the critical first day; in the egos of the participants, which came to occupy more and more of the battle to control the investigation as the publicity intensified; and the worst: the clear fact that there are two kinds of police procedures in America, one for the rich and another for the poor. Undoubtedly, there is not a police department in the United States who would have handled the JonBenét Ramsey case the way the Boulder officials handled it. The parents of any young child found dead under the same circumstances almost certainly would have been interrogated at once, in depth and separately, when the event was still horrific enough to have produced spontaneous answers. That did not happen in Boulder, and was why the investigation entered a state of seemingly terminal drift. It was a betrayal of our expectations about justice.

But for JonBenét Ramsey, the betrayal was final, and it was irredeemable.

Lisa Steinberg—six years old and defenseless, she was the brutalized victim of a couple's descent into delusion and violence.

Joel Steinberg—cruel and controlling, he ruled his family with intimidation and a deadly iron fist.

Hedda Nussbaum—beaten and brainwashed, did her loyalty to Joel keep her from saving Lisa—or was there a more disturbing reason?

Never before has a trial been so shocking, nor testimony so riveting. Here for the first time is the entire heart-rending story of an outwardly normal family living in the shadow of violence and fear, and the illegally adopted, innocent girl whose life was the price of affection. Retold in the framework of the sensational trial, it is a sad and gripping tale that stabs at the heart's tenderest core.

LISA, HEDDA & JOEL

The Steinberg Murder Case

Documented with 8 pages of gripping photographs

THE WORLD'S FOREMOST AUTHORITY
ON SERIAL KILLERS REVEALS THE FBI'S
ULTIMATE WEAPON AGAINST THE NATION'S
MOST DANGEROUS PSYCHOPATHS...
THEIR OWN MINDS.

Face-to-face with some of America's most terrifying killers, FBI veteran and ex-Army CID colonel Robert Ressler learned from them how to identify the unknown monsters who walk among us—and put them behind bars. Now the man who coined the phrase "serial killer" and advised Thomas Harris on *The Silence of the Lambs* shows how he is able to track down some of today's most brutal murderers.

WHOEVER FIGHTS MONSTERS

My Twenty Years Tracking Serial Killers for the FBI

Robert K. Ressler & Tom Shachtman